Blue

Social Fictions Series

Series Editor
Patricia Leavy
USA

The *Social Fictions* series emerges out of the arts-based research movement. The series includes full-length fiction books that are informed by social research but written in a literary/artistic form (novels, plays, and short story collections). Believing there is much to learn through fiction, the series only includes works written entirely in the literary medium adapted. Each book includes an academic introduction that explains the research and teaching that informs the book as well as how the book can be used in college courses. The books are underscored with social science or other scholarly perspectives and intended to be relevant to the lives of college students—to tap into important issues in the unique ways that artistic or literary forms can.

Please email queries to pleavy7@aol.com

Blue

Patricia Leavy

SENSE PUBLISHERS
ROTTERDAM / BOSTON / TAIPEI

A C.I.P. record for this book is available from the Library of Congress.

ISBN 978-94-6300-353-7 (paperback)
ISBN 978-94-6300-354-4 (hardback)
ISBN 978-94-6300-355-1 (e-book)

Published by: Sense Publishers,
P.O. Box 21858,
3001 AW Rotterdam,
The Netherlands
https://www.sensepublishers.com/

Printed on acid-free paper

PRAISE FOR *BLUE*

"I love it. I just love it. I wasn't planning on reading it this morning, but once I started, I couldn't stop. Tash is so familiar and yet unique. I get her discontents and I am rooting for her as soon as she says her first words. She's in New York City and I know she's going to make it. I want her to. And I want her friends, including the homeless man, to make it, too. In the accolades of the 1980s, I find the novel to be *cool, hip,* and *awesome*! It would be fantastic in any number of college courses. Young adults should read this. BRAVO, Patricia Leavy!" **Laurel Richardson, Ph.D., The Ohio State University**

"An engaging piece of public scholarship, *Blue* provides rich food for thought about the pop culture landscape and how its shapes our own stories. With a subtext about privilege, opportunity, sexual assault and gender, this would be a useful and fun teaching tool." **Sut Jhally, Ph.D., University of Massachusetts at Amherst; Founder & Executive Director, Media Education Foundation**

"*Blue* is a joyful, inspiring and painfully beautiful novel written by gifted scholar and writer, Patricia Leavy. *Blue* shows all of us how to move forward through times of pain, crisis or complacency with hope and love." **Norman Denzin, Ph.D., University of Illinois at Urbana-Champaign**

"*Blue* is a tour de force! Leavy shines her brightest in this little gem of a book. Authentic dialogue, fun but complex characters, and brilliant use of pop culture make this book a must-read. I don't want to give anything away, but the meaning of the title is genius. Beautiful! I love that we get to catch up with Tash from *Low-Fat Love* and be immersed in her sometimes endearing, sometimes frustrating, and all-too-relatable complexity again. The city is a refreshing character in this finely drawn book, transporting you to a hopeful, hip, vibrant New York. *Blue* inspires reflection and entertains. I highly recommend it!" **Amy Leigh Mercree, author of *The Spiritual Girl's Guide to Dating***

"*Blue*, Patricia Leavy's latest journey into social fiction, reminds me of what it meant to live through the *blue* of young adulthood, a time spent working through the complexities of a life that's constantly changing like the sky while struggling toward self-love, spiritual balance and happiness. Like *Low-Fat Love* I was immediately pulled in as a reader by Leavy's refreshing use of language, her descriptions helping me see the world she's creating, a world that feels as familiar as one I remember as if it were yesterday." **Mary E. Weems, Ph.D., author of *Blackeyed: Plays and Monologues* and Cleveland Arts Prize winner**

"Patricia Leavy's strength lies not just in writing relatable yet complex women, but also in the level of cultural and social research she puts into each page. *Blue* is more than a great read; it is the embodiment of sociological art, grounded in theory and method and mixed with all the fun pop culture has to offer. The result is stunning! I can't wait to use it in the classroom!" **Adrienne Trier-Bieniek, Ph.D., Valencia College**

"In her new novel *Blue*, Patricia Leavy maps the contemporary landscape of love by narrating a vibrant tale where complex and compelling characters dance with the possibilities of longing and romance like light and shadow dance a tango. Full of wisdom, wit, and wonder, swirling with vibrant voices that conjure the hope and loss we all know is the heart and truth of love, always more confounding than found, always calling us forth with indefatigable desire. *Blue* is a novel we all need to read now!" **Carl Leggo, Ph.D., University of British Columbia and Poet**

for beauty seekers everywhere,
and one in particular,
Celine Boyle

TABLE OF CONTENTS

FOREWORD

Patricia Leavy has done it again. Shimmering under a filmic haze of vintage mid-80s Greenwich Village, her latest novel *Blue* bursts to life with the elegance and electricity of a true New Yorker. Equal parts smart and funny, this book somehow also manages to be a love letter to anyone who has fallen in love, survived the death of a love affair, the death of a loved one, or walked with others through such profound loss. It is a work of immense empathy, a work of creative practice-led research about hope and loyalty, resilience and redemption.

Tash, Jason, and Penelope are characters we have all known or been. One of the innovations of this book is Leavy's decision to bring back Tash Daniels, the protagonist of her uber-popular book *Low-Fat Love,* the first in this Social Fictions series. *Blue* takes Social Fictions to a whole new level. Leavy's painful personal history and her well-publicized real-life muse, Tori Amos, have informed the creation of this latest novel, and Amos' artistry and lyricism are in evidence throughout, directly and indirectly. For this is ultimately a book about coming of age as a creative act, a book about family, and about the impossibility of living 'safe' lives. It shows the power of pop culture not only to reflect our experiences, but to co-create them. Leavy says, "the path through pain has always been creativity," and in this book readers will see that creative research finds its true validity in the affective authenticity of characters like us, and in this task *Blue* succeeds beyond measure.

Anne Harris, Ph.D.
Monash University
Australian Research Fellow in Creativity and Arts in Education

PREFACE

Blue follows three roommates as they navigate life and love in their post-college years. Tash Daniels, the former party girl, falls for deejay Aidan. Always attracted to the wrong guy, what happens when the right one comes along? Jason Woo, a lighthearted model on the rise, uses the club scene as his personal playground. While he's adept at helping Tash with her personal life, how does he deal with his own when he meets a man that defies his expectations? Penelope, a reserved and earnest graduate student slips under the radar, but she has a secret no one suspects. As the characters' stories unfold, each is forced to confront their life choices or complacency and choose which version of themselves they want to be. *Blue* is a novel about identity, friendship, and figuring out who we are during the "in-between" phases of life. The book shines a spotlight on the friends and lovers who become our families in the fullest sense of the word, and the search for people who "get us." The characters in *Blue* show how our interactions with people often bump up against backstage struggles we know nothing of. Visual art, television, and film appear as signposts throughout the narrative, providing a context for how we each come to build our sense of self in the world. With a tribute to 1980s pop culture, set against the backdrop of contemporary New York, *Blue* both celebrates and questions the ever-changing cultural landscape against which we live our stories, frame by frame.

The protagonist, Tash Daniels, originally appeared in my first novel, *Low-Fat Love* (*Blue* is set several years later). I found her a difficult character to like and enjoyed placing her story center stage, flaws and all. *Blue* follows Tash and a new set of characters and can be read as a stand-alone novel. For those who read *Blue* as a follow-up *to Low-Fat Love*, you will find some lingering questions are answered. *Low-Fat Love* explored women's identity construction in the context of isolation, low self-esteem, and destructive male figures; by contrast, *Blue* tackles questions about identity in the context of positive relationships.

Together, the novels represent two ends of a continuum, both suggesting the most important relationship we have is with ourselves. You needn't read anything else before you crack open these pages.

Although fictional, the novel is grounded in interview research, teaching, and personal observations, including my ongoing informal online communication with my students in their post-grad years. During the writing of this book, I immersed myself in 1980s pop culture and visited the locations in New York City that appear in the novel. In these ways, it can be considered arts-based research. Sociologically, the novel also highlights the disjuncture between what we see of people's lives and what they may be struggling with behind the scenes. *Blue* can be read entirely for pleasure or can be used as supplemental reading in a variety of courses in education, women's/gender studies, sociology, psychology, communication, popular culture, media studies, qualitative inquiry, narrative inquiry, or arts-based research.

I began writing *Blue* the day my daughter's biological father died after a long battle with cancer. I was home alone, trying to cope, and knew that for me, the path through pain has always been creativity. So I started writing what first came to my mind, simply as a way to get through the day. I created a handwritten list of all the colors flooding my mind. They were all shades of blue. A Tori Amos song called "Garlands" was playing the background. The song is set in New York City's Washington Square Park. Suddenly, I had a theme and location.

Although I had a different novel planned, *Blue* took on a life of its own, and I soon realized it was a book I was always meant to write. I pay tribute to the places in New York City I have loved the most, not because of the physical spaces themselves, but the hopefulness they inspired in me early in my life. I also give a nod to the pop culture that influenced me at critical moments in my life, to show how the pop culture we choose to consume becomes a part of who we are. Notwithstanding the grief that inspired me to start writing, or perhaps because of it, *Blue* is the most uplifting, humorous, and hopeful of all my books. At its core, it celebrates possibility. When it was finished, I began to think of it as a love letter to myself. I'm delighted to be able to share that love letter with others.

Patricia Leavy

ACKNOWLEDGEMENTS

First and foremost, thank you Peter de Liefde, publisher extra-ordinaire, for your faith in me and your willingness to support creativity. I am forever grateful to you and the entire team at Sense Publishers, particularly Paul Chambers for your tireless marketing efforts, Jolanda Karada for your outstanding production assistance, and Edwin Bakker and Robert van Gameren for your assistance getting copies out. Thank you to the editorial advisory board members of the *Social Fictions* series for your generosity, and to the early reviewers for your generous endorsements. Heartfelt thanks to Shalen Lowell, the world's best assistant and spiritual bodyguard. Thank you to Clear Voice Editing for the phenomenal copyediting services. Tori Amos, thank you for "Garlands" and "Oysters," which enabled me to crawl into a writing hole and come out the other side. To my Facebook community, I can only say thank you. I can't overstate how much your support has meant to me.

My deep gratitude to my friends and family, especially Ally Field, Monique Robitaille, Melissa Anyiwo, Pamela DeSantis, Mallory Sophronia, Anne Harris, Adrienne Trier-Bieniek, Mr. Barry Mark Shuman, Vanessa Alssid, and Carolyn and Charles Robins. Madeline Leavy-Rosen, love to you always. If you ever want to know who I am, aside from being your mom, read this. Mark Robins, you're the best spouse in the world. I couldn't do any of it without you. Dad, thanks for renting the movies I loved over and over again. You'll recognize them in these pages and hopefully see it wasn't a waste. Mom, thank you for the magical trips to New York when I was little and for giving me such incredible exposure to the art world. This book is a love letter to those places and what they inspired in me. Celine Boyle, you were the only person reading this as I was writing. Thank you for your invaluable feedback on every line and for "getting" me and my vision. You've made this book and my life so much better. Finally, for beauty seekers everywhere, and all those who are in love with love, books, and movies.

We are possibilities.

PART ONE

CHAPTER 1

That can't be right, Tash thought, squinting again to look at the time. "Shit," she said as she reached for the alarm clock. "Damn thing never works," she mumbled while placing it back on her nightstand. *I'm gonna be late again. I should hurry.* She rolled over before slowly stretching her arms and lazily dragging herself out of bed. Stumbling to her dresser and opening the top drawer, she rifled around for underwear before heading to the bathroom.

Twenty minutes later, wrapped in a towel after showering, she used her palm to wipe the steam from the mirror. *I look like crap. God, I hope I can cover those bags under my eyes,* she thought as she started to apply her signature black liquid eyeliner. *I'll use gray eyeshadow and make them smoky.* Realizing it must be getting late, she dried and straightened her long, dirty-blonde hair but skipped curling the ends to save time. Returning to her bedroom, she scoured her closet wondering what to wear before deciding on an off-the-shoulder, loose white tunic, a pair of skinny black jeans, and high-heeled black leather booties. Staring at herself in the mirror, she tried on four pairs of earrings, posing left and then right to fully view each option, before deciding on gold hoops. To match, she threw on her favorite gold, turquoise, and red evil-eye bracelet. *Coffee. I need coffee.*

En route to the galley kitchen, Tash stomped past her roommates' closed bedroom doors, clomping her heels without concern as to whether they were asleep. She got a bag of coffee and the nearly empty carton of milk out of the refrigerator, placed them on the counter, and opened the cupboard to get a coffee filter and her to-go tumbler, neither of which were there. She found her tumbler in the sink, dirty from the day before. *Fuck.* Turning back to focus on the coffee pot, she spotted a note sitting beside it. *There's nothing I dread first thing in the freaking morning more than these notes.*

Morning, Tash. Hope you didn't forget to turn the volume up on your alarm again and oversleep. I didn't want to wake you in case you had the day off. We're out of coffee filters and it's your turn to go to the store. I left my list on the back of this note. I can't cover for you this time so please go. Thanks. Have a nice day. Penelope

Tash flipped over the note and rolled her eyes. She started to leave the kitchen when she turned back, remembering to put the milk away. *Don't want the Gestapo after me for that again*, she thought. She headed into the common room, sans coffee, and looked around. *Where did I leave my bag?* The small loveseat was overflowing with random clothing, topped with her black blazer. *Hmm. Two pairs of men's shoes under the coffee table. Jason must have met someone. Good for him, but where's my stupid bag? Ah, there you are*, spotting her black bag hiding in the corner, with her keys and sunglasses conveniently lying on top of it. She scooped them up, put her dark glasses on, and headed out, double locking the door behind her.

"Hi, Mr. Collier," she said, passing her neighbor on the stairs.

"Good morning, Miss," he replied.

Despite the morning rush, she was able to hail a cab quickly. As the cab passed Washington Square Park, she stared at the chess players, already at it for the day. Soon she drifted into thoughts of the drama the day before. *Ray was a jerk, Jason was so right. He didn't deserve me. I'm glad I ended it.* As they pulled up to Alice & Olivia, Tash rummaged through her bag for cash before giving up and surrendering her credit card to the driver.

She flew into the store, quickly heading to the backroom before Catherine could open her mouth. Tash threw her arm up and hollered, "I know, and I'm sorry. My alarm didn't go off and blah, blah, blah."

"You're half an hour late, again," Catherine called after her.

"I know, I know, and I'm sorry," Tash said, rolling her eyes. As she hung her bag and blazer on a coat hook, Catherine continued to reprimand her.

"You need to get a new alarm clock then, because I..."

"I'll close for you tonight, okay? You can leave early; it's fine."

"You know if you left on time you could walk here and save yourself the cab fare. You probably lose at least an hour's wages by creating a situation in which you need to take a cab. And is it even faster with the morning traffic?"

As Catherine continued, Tash muttered under her breath, "Get off my ass, you bitch," if only to make herself feel better. She took a deep breath and headed to the Keurig machine to make some much-needed coffee. She plugged it in and flipped the switch, but Catherine exclaimed, "Don't bother. It broke yesterday." Tash squeezed her eyes shut, shook her head, and took another deep breath before forcing a smile onto her face. "Great, that's just great."

*

"I'm going to head out now, since you're closing tonight."

"Uh huh, fine Catherine. Have a good night," Tash said while leaning on the store counter and checking her phone. She was exchanging texts with Jason, reminding him to get them on the club list that weekend.

"Make sure you change the shoes and handbags in the window display. Last season's accessories go on sale tomorrow, so the newer items should be featured in the window."

"Uh huh," Tash said, without looking up from her phone.

"Okay, well, goodnight."

"Night, Catherine."

An hour later, after ringing up the final customers, Tash retrieved the new handbags and shoes from the backroom. She liked working on window displays because it was a chance to be creative and put things together in unexpected ways that were sure to perplex Catherine. Tash imagined the windows as still images from film, designed to convey a feeling as much as to display clothes. While there was a limit to what she could get away with, she pushed the bounds as much as possible. She didn't mind her job and loved working in SoHo, but window displays and the employee discount were the only aspects from which she derived genuine pleasure.

Once Tash was done putting accessories from the window onto the sale table, she gathered her things and locked up. With only a blazer on, she felt a chill. These early spring days were unusually warm but the evenings were still cold. *I should really walk home. I can't blow more money on a cab.* Desperate for a scarf, she stood on Greene Street rummaging through her slouchy leather hobo bag, which she carried everywhere despite its tendency to become a black hole in which she couldn't find anything. "Ah, there we go," she whispered as she pulled out a periwinkle scarf, which she double wrapped around her neck.

As the sky darkened, the SoHo lights seemed to shine at their brightest. Store windows screamed with flashing light bulbs, a frenetic attempt to command notice. Tash looked in the windows as she passed by, tempted by sale signs even though she was accustomed to them. These days, even New York City itself was on sale. Street vendors yearning to end their days well tried to entice her with sunglasses and other trinkets. When she smiled and shook her head, one guy screamed, "You look like Lindsay Lohan. You're dope."

"I get that a lot," she said with a mischievous smile.

As she crossed over into the Village, the restaurants and corner cafés were already bustling with people clamoring to sit outside. After a brutal winter, New Yorkers were ready to enjoy outdoor dining again. Waiters turned on heat lamps and uncorked wine bottles amid casual conversation and bubbling laughter.

Her feet sore, she slowed her pace as she passed Washington Square Park. As day turned to night, the park was the center of the world around her. People from all walks of life appeared. The parade of artists, writers, students, homeless people, drug dealers, professors, tourists, and countless others made it the perfect microcosm of the city itself, the dream and its shadow side. She overheard a group of preppy college students talking about social justice as they passed Harold, actively trying not to notice as he set up his sleeping bag on a bench. *Jerks*, she thought. *They're such posers.*

A year earlier, Tash had twisted her ankle racing to work one morning. A barrage of f-bombs flew out of her mouth. Harold, a witness to the accident, helped her to a bench and told her not to curse.

"Are you for real?" she asked.

"It's undignified," he replied. "Do you think you can walk?"

"Uh, yeah, but not in these shoes."

They spoke for a few more minutes before she decided to stumble back to her apartment to ice her ankle and change shoes. Since that day, she'd say hi to Harold when she saw him and stopped to talk with him at least once every couple of weeks, usually bringing him a cup of coffee and sometimes a donut. Powdered sugar was his favorite.

He once started to tell his life story and she interrupted saying, "It's cool, Harold. We don't have to do this. I don't need you to explain." He seemed relieved. Since then, their conversations were usually about how they were each doing that particular day. Although routinely chased away by the police, he always returned. On this night, she just waved as she passed him.

Only half a block from her apartment, she had the horrible realization that she was supposed to get groceries. Not willing to endure a lecture from Penelope, she passed her apartment building and headed to the corner grocer. After grabbing a hand basket and making a beeline to the freezer for some ice cream, she started searching for Penelope's grocery list. As she fumbled for the list, mumbling, "Ah, where is that stupid thing?" she heard a voice say,

"Maybe you'd have better luck if you shut your eyes and put your hand in."

"Huh?" she queried, looking up at the six-foot-tall guy standing before her, dressed from head to toe in black. He had bleached blonde spiky hair, high cheekbones, a strong jawline, and a piercing through his right eyebrow that she thought was simultaneously cool and disgusting.

"You know, sometimes if you're looking too hard, you can't find anything."

"Uh, yeah," she said, staring into his evergreen eyes. *Oh my God, he's seriously hot.*

"Here, tell me what you're looking for and I'll shut my eyes and stick my hand in for you."

Raising her eyebrows, she said, "How stupid do you think I am? Maybe I should just go outside and scream, 'Somebody rob me!'"

He laughed. "Fair enough, but you try it."

Tash smirked and stuck her hand into her bag without looking. "Uh huh, here it is!" she exclaimed as she pulled out the small, crumpled paper. "That's uncanny."

"Sometimes you just have to concentrate less, you know?" he said. "What's so important, anyway?"

"Oh, it's just my roommate's grocery list. She's pretty uptight so I can't screw it up. You wouldn't believe the things she writes, like 'two organic red apples and flax seed powder,' whatever the hell that is. Anyway, I should probably get back to shopping."

He smiled and waved his arm, to indicate she could pass by. With only a few aisles in the small store, Tash bumped into him again in the produce section.

"Should I even ask what that's about?" she said while giggling, looking at the twenty or more coconuts in his basket.

"Oh, these are for a party I'm deejaying for a couple of friends over at NYU."

"They're serving whole coconuts?" she asked, mystified.

He laughed. "People try to get them open. It's like a drinking game kind of thing. It's pretty funny."

"Gotcha. Do you go to NYU?"

"No, I went to school in Chicago and moved to New York after I graduated. I'm a professional deejay. I'm just doing this party as a favor."

"So, what kinds of clubs do you spin at?" she asked.

"Uh, well, tomorrow I'll be spinning at the Forever 21 store in Times Square."

She smiled. "Well, do you get a discount at least?"

He laughed. "Didn't think to ask for that. So, what's your name?"

"Natashya, but my friends call me Tash."

"I'm Aidan. Do you live around here?"

"Just a block away. I share a place with two roommates."

"Pretty awesome area to live in, good for you."

"Yeah, well we're in like the only non-restored building in the neighborhood. Don't get me wrong, I love living here and it's pretty close to my work, but we're not in one of the swanky buildings with a marble entrance. It's more like splintery wood floors and a scary old-fashioned elevator that makes me want to take the stairs."

He smiled. "What's your work?"

"I work at a couple of stores in SoHo."

"For the discount, right?" he said with a smirk.

Tash laughed. "Well, nice to meet you but I've gotta finish up and get going."

"Sure, me too. Maybe I'll see you around. If you're not busy, stop by Forever 21 tomorrow."

"I have to work."

"Well, can I maybe get your number?" he asked.

"Why don't you give me yours instead?"

"Sure, that's cool." He put his coconut-filled basket on the ground and held out his hand. "Give me your phone and I'll put it in."

"You don't want me to have to search my bag again. Here," she said, handing him the note with Penelope's grocery list. "Do you have a pen?"

Aidan smiled and pulled a red crayon out of his pocket. "Don't ask," he said as he wrote his number on the little paper. "Here," he said handing it to her. "See ya."

"See ya," she said.

When she casually glanced around the store a few minutes later, he was gone. She brought her basket to the checkout. The cashier asked, "Did you find everything you needed?"

"Yeah, yeah I did."

*

Her feet aching and her arms overloaded, Tash felt like she was going to drop by the time she made it home. She dumped her handbag and keys on the entryway floor and swung the shopping bags onto the kitchen counter. She opened her new box of popcorn and stuck a packet in the microwave before putting the rest of the groceries away. She giggled to herself, thinking about the coconuts filling Aidan's basket. *I wonder if Jason is home.*

Tash met Jason Woo at a club a few years earlier. She was having trouble getting past the bouncers when Jason came to her rescue. His modeling career was just starting to take off thanks to landing a gig as Calvin Klein's first Asian male model. Both sarcastic and carefree, they bonded immediately and moved in together as soon as Tash graduated from college. Though they had a hard time looking out for themselves, they did a remarkable job of looking out for each other.

Tash was so lost in thought about Aidan's coconuts that she didn't hear Jason approaching.

"Hey," Jason said from the doorway.

"Oh, hey." She tossed him a bag of coffee. "Stick that in the fridge." As he put the coffee away, Tash said, "This too," and flung the loaf of bread.

"I can't believe you actually went shopping. Did Pen leave you one of her famous notes?"

"Yup," she said just when the microwave beeped. "Is she in her room studying?"

"She's not here. I think she had dinner plans with her study group or something."

"Seriously? She's unbelievable, making me do all this when she's not even here," she said as she opened the popcorn bag. Steam burned her hand and caused her to drop the bag on the counter. "Fuck," she mumbled.

"How is it you never learn not to open it that way?" Jason asked facetiously. "Here, I got it," he said. He grabbed a bowl from the cupboard and emptied the bag for her.

"You know if you leave it in the bag it's one less dish to wash. That's why I do that."

"Since when do you ever wash the dishes anyway?" he rebuffed, as he ate a handful of her popcorn.

"I don't know why she made me go to the store if she wasn't even gonna be home," Tash said as she threw the two empty grocery bags in the garbage.

"I know you can't relate, but some people actually plan ahead. She probably wanted breakfast."

"Oh, right, like you plan ahead," Tash jabbed, tossing a jar of maraschino cherries.

"You're lucky I caught that. What is it with you and these things?" he asked, sticking them in the door of the refrigerator.

"You know I love them. I can't help it," she said. "But listen, I kind of met a guy. I met him at the store while I was getting Pen's crap, so maybe it was meant to be."

"You met a guy? Ah, do tell," he prodded.

"Well from the looks of things this morning, I'm guessing you also met a guy, so you tell first." She opened the refrigerator and grabbed two cans of Diet Coke.

"Some lighting guy from the shoot. I kicked him out this morning."

"You're such a slut. Must be hard to be so irresistible," Tash bemused.

Jason smiled. "You would know. Come on, let's go curl up on my bed and you can tell me all about the guy you met. I hope he's better than Ray. I'm eating half this popcorn, by the way," he said, taking a fistful and heading to his room.

"Hey, that's my dinner!"

CHAPTER 2

Two afternoons a week, Tash worked at Anna Sui, which was directly across the street from Alice & Olivia. She was friends with one of the saleswomen, Isabelle, an aspiring actress who needed afternoons free for auditions and hooked her up with the job.

When the store was quiet, Tash was supposed to dust the glass display cases filled with jewelry and wallets or flatten old shoeboxes in preparation for the recycling company. Instead, she frequently used one of the tester nail polishes on the front counter to give herself a manicure. She loved how the bottles were shaped like a woman dressed in a black bustier. *The gold sparkle is definitely better than the silver*, Tash thought as she admired her nail lacquer. She leaned her elbows on the counter, blowing gently to dry her newly polished nails.

Her nails were still tacky when her phone beeped on the counter beside her. She peered over to read the incoming text from Jason:

> All set on the list tom night. But no shots for u tequila girl. Xx

She replied:

> Hey, any chance u could add one more? Xx

Fuck, I smudged my nail, she muttered, scrutinizing her right hand as she waited for a response.

> For Coconut Boy I presume? Who's the slut now? Yeah, can do. U owe me. U pain in the ass. xx

Next, she texted Aidan, having saved his number the night before, just in case.

```
Hey.  It's  Tash  from  the  store  last
night.
```

Before she could put the phone down it beeped. *That's eager*, she thought.

```
Hey.  So  now  I  have  your  #.  Setting  up
at  4ever21.  Times  Sq.  =  insanity.  Can
you  swing  by?
```

She waited a minute before responding.

```
Gonna  pass  on  the  neon  signs  +  mobs  of
tweens.  Must  be  good  4  your  self-esteem
2  spin  Katy  Perry's  greatest  hits  4  the
kiddies.  Bet  the  girls  looove  u.
```

Only a moment passed before her phone beeped again.

```
Ah,  so  I  see  we're  already  up  to  the
mockery  part  of  this  relationship.  Ok
smart  ass,  u  tell  me.  What's  next?
```

As she started to laugh, she heard the annoying bell on the store door and the chatter of customers. "Please let me know if I can be of any help," she said unenthusiastically as they passed by.

She texted her response to Aidan quickly, smudging another nail.

```
My  roommate  got  us  on  the  list  at  Y  tom
night.  Can  get  u  on  2.10pm.
```

"Miss, can you open this case please?" one of the customers hollered from the back of the store.

"I'll be right there, ma'am."

```
Cool.  C  u  there.  A.
```

Smitten, she leaned on to the counter to daydream when she remembered the customer in the back. "Shit," she mumbled as she jumped up and grabbed the shop keys from beside the register.

"On my way, ma'am."

*

Although she told Aidan to meet her outside the club at ten o'clock, Tash and Jason arrived at ten thirty. There were throngs of over- and underdressed bodies, fighting for their place behind the velvet rope, without realizing that even if they made it behind the rope there was little hope of actually getting into the club that night. Tash knew those hopefuls didn't stand a chance and she loved blowing past them, pretending her privilege was so grand it even prevented her from recognizing her special status. Jason was her ticket to that particular euphoria. Despite the mob scene, Tash spotted Aidan immediately, nonchalantly standing slightly outside of the crowd. With Jason in tow, she grabbed him and without a word spoken, the three waltzed into the club, with a mere nod exchanged between Jason and the bouncer.

They reached the main bar on the far side of the club before Tash stopped. With the music blaring, they stood close together and Tash shouted, "Aidan, this is Jason. Jason, Aidan."

"Hey man, thanks for hooking me up," Aidan said with an outstretched hand.

Jason shook his hand. "No worries." He then turned to Tash and said, "You all good?"

"Yeah, thanks sweetie," she said as she leaned in and pecked his cheek. "Go do your thing and I'll see you at home, or not."

"Later. Be good!" With that, Jason disappeared into the crowd.

Before Aidan could say anything, Tash asked, "So, do you want a drink?"

"Hello to you too," he said with a chuckle. "I'll get them. What do you want?"

"Tequila sunrise."

"That makes sense."

"What does that mean?"

"Tequila sunrise: hardcore but flirty. Totally you."

Tash smirked.

"Forgive me, I've bartended. You start to see patterns."

"So if I hadn't told you what I wanted, what would you have guessed?"

"Tequila sunrise."

Tash smiled. "Okay, very cute smart boy. Now go get my drink."

"You got it. And by the way, you look amazing." When Aidan returned with her drink, he said, "Cheers," and clinked his glass to hers.

"Cheers," she said before taking a gulp. "Wowza, that's strong. What's that?" she asked, gesturing to his glass.

"Club soda."

"Club soda? Just club soda?"

"Club soda with lime. I don't drink."

"Alcoholic?" she asked with a hint of hopefulness.

He shook his head. "Nope, just don't drink."

"You don't look like a straight edge."

"Well, then I'm already surprising you. That's good, right? I mean, for a girl who I bet gets bored easily."

She couldn't help but smile. "So when you're spinning at parties and coming up with crazy drinking games, you're stone-cold sober?"

"That's why my games are so good."

Tash nearly finished her drink as they looked around. There was a lot to take in. The club boasted a mammoth dance floor with platforms that people could jump up on when they wanted to be noticed, as well as bars on every side. Dozens of strobe lights and black iron chandeliers draped with crystals and purple light bulbs pulsed in sync with the techno music. Like Tash and Aidan, most people were dressed in black. Drag queens in long, sequined, jewel-colored gowns stood at the edges of the bars passing out cheap feather boas for twenty bucks a pop.

Aidan leaned over to Tash as she took another swig of her drink. "Is this a gay club? It's cool, I'm just curious."

"No, it's just gay-friendly," Tash said.

"Do you want to dance?"

"Sure." She grabbed his glass and said, "I'll ditch these. Be right back." She returned a moment later and soon they were on the corner of the dance floor, jumping, spinning, and swaying along with everyone. Aidan never took his eyes off her and every once in a while she smirked. They danced for hours, only taking breaks to use the bathroom or when Tash wanted another drink.

Late in the evening, when Tash returned from a trip to the bathroom, Aidan draped a white boa around her neck. She smiled and he said, "It gets better. Come here. Working in the deejay circuit has its advantages. And by the way, if you ever want to get onto a club list, I can hook you up."

He pulled her onto the dance floor, and within moments, a remix of ABBA's "Dancing Queen" came on. She finally broke down and laughed hysterically. Everyone around them jumped and cheered as loose feathers from all the boas flew in the air, falling around them like the sparkles in the snow globes she loved as a child. Tash pulled Aidan to her and leaned into him. They held each other and swayed as feathers landed in their hair.

*

The next morning, wearing black palazzo pants and a bra as she searched for a top, Tash heard a gentle tap on her bedroom door. She threw the clothes she was holding onto her bed and opened the door to find Jason holding two mugs of coffee.

"You're the best," she said as she snagged one.

Jason stood in the open doorway, scanning the room with a mischievous look on his face. "No Coconut Boy?" he queried.

"Oh shush. Come help me choose an outfit."

Jason plopped himself on her bed.

"What do you think of this?" she asked, holding up a sparkly top.

He shook his head, took a sip of coffee, and said, "I think I drank too much for that. The one over there is better."

She slipped on the simple white tank top he pointed to and stood in front of her dresser holding various hoop earrings to each ear. After she settled on the larger pair, Jason said, "Seriously, I expected you to steal my coffee for Coconut Boy. No sleepover? He was hot. Very Billy Idol in his heyday, but taller."

"I'm meeting him later."

"Wow, you didn't give it up on the first night. I'm impressed. You must like him."

"Oh shut up. I'm just not a slut like you."

"Yes you are," he said, sipping his coffee. "Ooh, speaking of sluts, Pen didn't come home last night."

"Oh please, she probably fell asleep at the library," Tash said as she applied her lip gloss. He laughed.

She sat on the edge of the bed, zipping up her black platform booties.

"So where are you meeting him?"

"I'm working a half-day and then meeting him at the MoMA."

"Wow!" he exclaimed, his eyes widening. "You must really like him to take him to your special place. Good for Coconut Boy."

"Please stop calling him that."

"Ooh, you reeeally like him."

"We just needed a place to meet, drama queen."

"Uh huh, sure."

"Oh screw you," she said as she leaned over and kissed his head.

"Screw you too, bitch."

She grabbed her purse, threw her hand up, and said, "Later, sweetie."

*

Aidan jumped up when he saw her. Before he could say anything, she blurted out, "Hey, I know. I'm sorry. I'm not always late, really."

"I already know that's not true," he said with a laugh. "No worries. Should we get tickets?"

"My membership will get us both in."

"Cool. Shall we?" he asked, putting his hand out.

"You're so corny, straight edge," she said as she took his hand.

They walked hand-in-hand. Aidan leaned over and whispered, "You know, your bullshit doesn't fool me, beauty queen."

She leered at him, but her eyes sparkled. As they headed up the escalator, she said, "Let's start at the top and work our way down. My favorite spot is on the second floor and I want to save it."

"If I'm worthy, right?"

"You're worthy."

*

The top floor boasted a special exhibit that paired the "blue" works of Picasso and Miró: paintings from Picasso's Blue Period and a sampling of Miró's greatest pieces, including his three-part masterpiece, Triptych Bleu I, II, III.

"Picasso is one of my favorites," Aidan said, "but the Blue Period is so dark. It isn't even just sad, you know, it's bleak. I'm not afraid of the dark side, but this is pretty far down the rabbit hole."

"Well, his friend offed himself and he was depressed."

"The people look like such sad souls, isolated and alone."

"I think it's their loneliness that makes them so wretched. I mean look at this one," Tash said, stopping in front of a portrait of a woman. "She's one of the prostitutes he painted. A rare moment of solitude. She probably wasn't alone much."

"But you don't need to be alone to be lonely, right?" Aidan said.

"True." They continued their tour, and when they reached the room devoted to Miró's Triptych Bleu, they stopped to take it in.

"It's amazing how one color can convey so many different emotions. Is there anything more cheerful than this? He was so playful," Tash remarked.

"I have to admit, I don't necessarily understand what he was doing, but I think it's awesome," Aidan replied.

"Yeah, it makes sense to me, but not in a way I can explain with words."

Aidan nodded, and then walked to the corner of the room to read the curator's notes. When he returned he said, "It says that Miró thought blue was the color of the unconscious and the surreal, like a dream state."

"That's probably why it makes sense even though it like doesn't. You know? It taps into something that we get deep down."

"Totally," Aidan agreed.

"You know I never do that, look at what they write."

"Why?" he asked.

"It clouds how you see it. This might sound strange, but when I look at a painting and I start to get it, the images move, you know like a little film. It's like the film shows me what it means."

"That's not strange; it's awesome and I get it. I sort of have that with music. I see things, like objects or people doing something from a distance, and then I start to hear them."

She smiled. "Even when I was little, before I studied film, I did that."

"So if you don't read in museums, how do you know that Picasso's Blue Period was inspired by his friend's suicide?"

"I said I don't read the curator shit. I didn't say I don't read at all, genius."

Aidan blushed and looked down. "Fair enough, beauty queen."

"Okay, let's move it along," she said, taking his hand. He chuckled and they continued through the exhibit.

"I know a few things too," he said. "Did you know that Cézanne supposedly had at least sixteen shades of blue on his palette when he painted?"

"The guy who painted fruit?" she asked.

"Uh huh."

"Yeah, I knew that."

Aidan blushed and looked down again.

"But how about when he started painting skulls instead of apples and pears? Talk about dark. Maybe all that blue got to him after all," she said with a wry laugh.

"Yeah, maybe. Nothing gets past you. You know who should be known for his blue stuff? Chagall."

"I was never really into him. Did he use a lot of blue?"

"At the Art Institute in Chicago there are these amazing stained glass windows that Chagall created, cobalt blue with all sorts of symbols about America. They're pretty cool and there's always a flock of people standing in front of them."

"Aren't those in *Ferris Bueller's Day Off*? You know, in the museum scene?"

"Leave it to you to turn visual art into a movie," he said.

"I'm obsessed with all things eighties these days, especially movies."

"Cool. They kiss in front of the Chagall windows, Ferris and Sloane."

"She was so pretty. I wanted to be her in that time. I wonder what happened to that actress."

"She's got nothing on you. Funny how that kissing scene casually comes up in conversation, and we just happen to be in a museum and all."

"Okay, smart boy. Let's move it along."

By the time they reached the next floor, talk of art faded and they shared the details of their lives. Painting by painting, floor by floor, they talked about their childhoods, families, and what brought them to New York.

*

Tash learned that Aidan grew up in a small, middle-class suburb in the Midwest, in a home that his lower-middle-class parents struggled to afford. Although he clearly had a loving family, he was a misfit from an early age in a town that "prioritized football and God, in that order." In grade school he often found himself alone, lost in graphic novels and music, "imagining the beats of the music were footsteps, marching me away from that place."

He told her he was always the kid wearing headphones because they provided a protective bubble that no one could puncture. He lived in a sonic world when the real world let him down. Thanks to his height, which had him towering over many of the jocks, he was rarely bullied. Things changed in high school when his good looks and charisma propelled him into popularity with the girls. On several occasions when he was walking home alone at night after studying in the library, he was jumped by a group of jocks. They did little damage but always left a mark, like a fat lip or black eye. Despite his attempts to conceal his injuries or lie about their origin, his mother worried terribly and became critical of his gothic dress and "attention-getting" piercings. It put stress on his home life.

"Suddenly, who I was became a problem," he explained.

Tash asked, "If they only attacked you when you walked home at night, why didn't you just study at home or get a friend to walk with you?"

"Acquiescing to fear is a dangerous road. I guess I wasn't going to walk down it and give them that kind of control over me. I knew it would never be that bad. But you know what really got me? Every time they'd come after me, they'd call me gay. I know that it was a catch-all insult for those misogynist fucks, but come on. They're beating me up for fucking their girlfriends while they call me gay? Even as they hit me, I was laughing on the inside."

"They weren't very creative, that's for sure. Pathetic dicks."

"They said it so frequently that sometimes I wondered if they really believed it and they were just confused about why they hated me. Getting into the world of deejaying in Chicago was my way out of that small-minded crap. New York was the next stop. I'm making a name for myself on the circuit."

"Yeah, I kinda gathered that last night," she said, looking down sheepishly.

He smiled.

"Wanna hear something really messed up?"

He nodded.

"When I was in college, I studied abroad in Amsterdam."

"Don't tell me, you picked Amsterdam for the pot?"

"No, to work in the Red Light District," she said with a straight face.

He just looked at her.

"I'm kidding, God. I went to The University of Amsterdam for a semester because they have a kickass film studies program. Plus, you know, the pot."

He laughed.

"So I'm in Amsterdam during orientation and they set up all of these activities to help us get to know each other and the city and stuff. I signed up for a boat tour. A big-time feminist, Gender in Film professor took us. So we're on the boat and the automated guide is blaring out information like, 'look left to see whatever.' We all turn to see the famous thing, and there is this chick up against a wall, like my age, and this guy is screwing her. I mean, his pants are around his ankles and he's got her pinned against the wall, holding her wrists."

"Oh my God."

"But here's the messed up part: everyone just watches and the professor shouts, "He's fucking her! He's totally fucking her!" And we all just watched until the boat was too far away to see them anymore. To this day, I don't know if they were having public sex or if he was raping her. I can picture it clear as day and still don't know what to think. How could they all be so sure it was consensual, or did they just not care? Voyeuristic fucks. Sick. It was never mentioned again, not by the professor or anyone."

Aidan stopped walking, turned to Tash, and said, "That's really horrible."

"My point is that sometimes people don't know what to think about what they're seeing or feeling. They pick a reaction and go with it, even if it really doesn't make sense. It's all they're capable of. Even when they're right in the middle of it, sometimes they don't know. Like with those assholes who beat on you for screwing their girls while they called you gay."

He leaned in and gave her a soft, quick kiss on her lips. They continued walking, loosely holding hands, as if entirely natural.

*

As the escalator reached the second floor, Tash pulled Aidan along. "Come on."

"Wow, this is cool," Aidan said as they entered a large space with eight different parts of a film being projected onto the walls.

"Shh," Tash said, as she tugged him.

Cushions lined the edges of the room and large bean bags and pillows filled the center of the space. People were sitting all over the place watching the moving images.

Tash spotted an empty cushion in the far corner of the room and led Aidan there. From that vantage point, they could see most of the installments.

Tash leaned over and whispered, "It's this genius Japanese filmmaker. She won an international competition and got a huge grant when she was still in grad school. It was supposed run as a special exhibit, but that was over a year ago. It's like temporarily permanently here. It's about energy, about nature and humans. She filmed it in at least four Asian countries, and the images are incredible. It's the cinematography that I really love. Just watch. You'll get it."

People came and went, but an hour later, Tash and Aidan were still sitting there, leaning on the wall and each other.

Eventually Aidan whispered, "It's mesmerizing. I could stay here forever."

"Yeah, me too."

They looked at each other and he leaned in and kissed her. With his hand holding her face and beautiful images floating all around them, she felt entirely content.

*

The next morning, Tash awoke to realize she was cradled in Aidan's arms. She tried to wriggle her way out without disturbing him, but as soon as she moved, he sighed.

"Good morning," he said groggily.

She sat up and said, "Hey, sorry. I didn't mean to wake you."

"That's okay. What are you doing?"

"I need to shower."

"So you got what you want and now you're done with me. Is that it?" he asked sarcastically.

Expressionless, she turned to face him. "Yup, that's it."

"Come on, beauty queen," he whispered as he rubbed her arm. "Don't run away. Get back over here." He pulled her down and started tickling her while taunting, "Can you take it? Can you keep a straight face?"

Soon she was laughing hysterically. "I give in. I give in!"

He stopped tickling her and gently wiped her hair away from her eyes. "You're beautiful. Last night, well…"

Before he could finish, she leapt up and said, "Yeah, yeah, yeah, but without a shower and coffee, I'm gonna be a mega bitch."

He looked down and smiled coyly. "Coffee would be good."

Tash wrapped herself in her robe while Aidan threw on his T-shirt and boxers.

"Come on. Let's see if Jason's up and then you can meet my other roommate."

They passed Jason's bedroom and saw the door was wide open. "Looks like someone didn't come home last night," Tash muttered.

Just when they approached the kitchen, Penelope was catching her bagel as it popped up from the toaster. She fumbled a bit and dropped it on the counter. Tash wasn't sure if the bagel was hot or if they had startled her.

"Good morning, Tash."

"Hey. This is Aidan."

"Hey," Aidan said.

Penelope brushed her long, loose curls away from her face, adjusted her glasses, and nodded in acknowledgment.

"We were just gonna make coffee. Do you want some?" Tash asked.

"Oh, no thanks. I made this to take with me. I have plans and I'm already late."

Tash was no longer paying attention. She loaded a filter with coffee grounds as Aidan waited in the doorway.

Penelope wrapped her bagel in a napkin and scooted past Aidan.

"Nice to meet you," he called after her.

"You too."

Tash turned to Aidan and gave him an exaggerated eye roll. She opened her mouth but he put his finger against his lips and turned his head to watch Penelope leave the apartment.

The door clicked shut and Tash opened her mouth, but was again derailed when Jason came in.

"Hey," Aidan said.

"Oh, hey Aidan."

"I'm in here," Tash called. "We're making coffee. Want some?"

"No, I'm gonna crash for a while," he replied as he made his way through the small, crowded space.

"I need to go text my friend about something. I'll be right back," Aidan said before making himself scarce.

"See ya man," Jason said.

As soon as Aidan was out of earshot, Jason turned to Tash. "So, you and Coconut Boy must have had a good time yesterday."

"Oh, shut up you slut. What boy's heart did you break when you abandoned him this morning?"

"Well, at least I stayed until the morning," he said, opening the refrigerator.

"Yeah, what's up with that?" Tash asked.

"I had one too many shots and staying over just seemed easier."

She laughed.

Empty-handed, he shut the refrigerator and said, "Pen passed by me without even taking a beat for a hello. Where's she running off to?"

"Who the hell knows? Probably the library. You should have seen her face when she saw Aidan. It was so funny."

"He does look pretty fine in his skivvies."

"How much do you want to bet that Pen leaves me a note asking me to cover him up better? Little miss propriety."

"She's not that bad. Just remember, without her, you and I would need to be the grown-ups."

Tash smiled.

"I'm going to crash. Say goodbye to Coconut Boy for me."

"His name is Aidan."

He smirked. "Say goodbye to Aidan for me."

CHAPTER 3

Later that night as Tash lay in bed, Aidan's scent still on her sheets, images from the night before played in her mind. His eyes locked onto hers, his soft lips, and the firm press of his flesh, their bodies entangled. It was so good she could hardly remember it all, just a jumble of flickering moments and sensations etched in her memory. Over and over again, she imagined the feel of his touch and the look in his eyes. *Fuck. What's wrong with me? It was just good sex. Really good sex. Don't be one of those idiots who loses it because of an orgasm. Get a grip.* But no matter how hard she tried, whenever her mind quieted it was flooded with memories of how she felt lost in his eyes. Then, she had a surprising realization. *Shit, I don't usually open my eyes with guys. Why did we do that? What was that? New cardinal rule: no orgasms with open eyes. Messes with your brain.* She rolled over to go to sleep. As she drifted off, she pulled the sheets up high, clinging to the faint smell of him.

The next morning, she woke up to a text from Aidan.

Hey beautiful. When can I see u?

Not wanting to appear overly available, she showered, flipped through a magazine, and ate breakfast before responding.

No plans today.

Spinning at the H&M on 5th until 6. Meet me?

She laughed and thought, I could use some tights anyway.

Sure. Will be fun to see your groupies.

Tash arrived at H&M at five thirty. Aidan was set up just inside the store's entrance. Although he was wearing large black headphones and was engrossed in the music, he acknowledged her immediately with a wide smile. She made a funny face and he looked down, blushing. She pointed to the accessories on the far wall and he nodded, continuing with his work. No matter where she was in the store, whenever she looked back at Aidan, he had his eyes on her. Twenty minutes later, she returned with a small plastic bag containing her new tights and a belt. She walked over to Aidan, pecked him on the cheek, and sat on the edge of the display case near him. She sat back among the mannequins and watched nearly everyone checking Aidan out, girls and guys alike. While some women might feel insecure that a stream of people were admiring and even flirting with the person they're seeing, Tash reveled in it. *He can hold his own*, she thought.

Aidan gestured that he was shutting it down after one last tune. He transitioned from techno to a remix of "Dancing Queen." She put her hand on her chest, bowed her head, and laughed, overjoyed. When the song was over, he took his headphones off, turned to her and said, "I planned that one for you."

"Yeah, I sorta got that," she said, blushing.

"Want to make sure I keep surprising you."

You are, she thought.

Tash fiddled with her phone while Aidan packed up. Soon, he threw his backpack on and said, "Ready if you are."

As they headed out onto a bustling Fifth Avenue, Tash asked, "Where do you want to go?"

"Have you seen *Kinky Boots*, the musical?"

She shook her head. "But I do have a secret Cyndi Lauper girl crush."

He smiled. "I don't want you to think it's always gonna be like this because there's no way I can usually afford this kind of thing. A buddy of mine works on the show; he's been promising me tickets for ages and finally came through."

"Is he an actor?"

"Lighting guy. Nothing glamorous but it comes with perks. He called earlier and said if we get there fifteen minutes before the show, he has a couple of balcony seats for us. You in?"

"Fuck yeah."

"You know you have a real potty mouth," he said jokingly.

"Oh fuck, your Midwestern upbringing?"

He laughed. "No, I dig it. They say cursing is a sign of honesty."

"Well, don't believe everything you fucking hear."

"I'll keep that in mind, beauty queen. Come on, let's head down fifty-second to cut over," he said, grabbing her hand and guiding her.

On the way to Times Square, Tash teased Aidan about his "groupies." When they passed the MoMA, he gently squeezed her hand. They decided to stop at Aidan's favorite sandwich shop for a quick bite before the show, but as they got closer to the neon signs and Broadway lights, Aidan stopped against a building and handed his backpack to Tash.

"Hold this for a sec," he said as he unzipped it and pulled out his iPod and large headphones. "Put these on."

She looked at him quizzically.

"It's a new remix I'm working on. It's inspired by something I saw on the Times Square Midnight Moment – you know, the big arts campaign that uses the billboard space for digital art."

She nodded. "I've seen it."

"I want you to listen to it as you walk into Times Square."

She put the headphones on and Aidan pressed play before tucking the iPod into her pocket. He put his backpack on, grabbed her hand, and zipped towards the epicenter. Her heart raced as the music kicked in. Everything was vibrating: the ground, her skin, the neon signs begging for attention. She felt like she was racing through a film. Suddenly Aidan made a sharp right turn and pulled her into an old-fashioned sandwich shop. He took the headphones off her head and the clamor of human sounds in mundane conversation returned.

"You look flushed," he said. "What did you think?"

"Incredible rush. It was like you created the soundtrack for my energy mixing with the city's energy."

He leaned over and kissed her. "Come on, there are a couple of seats at the end of the counter."

They snagged the seats and Tash looked up at the menu board.

An older waitress with dyed red hair came over. "What can I get you?"

"You first," Tash said.

"Steak and cheese, no peppers please."

"Something to drink?"

"I'm good with water. Thanks."

"I'll have a grilled cheese and tomato on the challah bread and just water. Thanks," Tash said.

"I discovered this place when I had my first gig in the area. Killer sandwiches. We were lucky to get a couple of stools; it's usually packed so I have to eat on the go."

"Your music is really amazing. After that first drop, I felt like I took off. I don't know how else to describe it. It was like it injected me into the cityscape."

He blushed. "Thanks. After seeing that film installation at the MoMA, I knew you'd get it."

"Jason's the only other person I've taken to see that. Most people I know wouldn't appreciate it."

"You two must be really close."

"Yeah, he's my person, you know?"

"He seems chill. What's he like?"

"He's a really good guy, very smart. People see that he's hot and funny and miss out on all of his best qualities. He's so often the center of attention that people don't realize he holds back most of who he is. He's careful about what he chooses to let people in on."

The waitress returned and slid their plates in front of them.

"Always super fast here," Aidan said as he took a couple of napkins from the dispenser and handed one to Tash.

She picked up her sandwich and pulled apart the two halves, watching the cheese ooze. "This was my favorite when I was a kid. But I didn't know about challah bread until I came to New York." She took a big, uninhibited bite. "That's so good," she said as she chewed, the gooey cheese mixing with the buttery toast.

Aidan smiled and dug into his sandwich.

When they finished eating, the waitress dropped off the bill and Tash quickly took it. "I got this," she said and threw down some money. He thanked her and they headed to the show.

When they arrived at the theater, Tash stood in line while Aidan picked up their tickets at Will Call. They found their second-row balcony seats and marveled at their good fortune. Aidan offered Tash a program and she shook her head.

"Of course, you don't want it to spoil it."

"Exactly."

They stood up to let an elderly couple pass by. The couple sat beside Tash, and the man asked his wife, "What's this about?" She replied, "It's about the gays, but it's supposed to be excellent." Tash shot a sideways glance at Aidan and they giggled discreetly at each other. Moments later, the lights went out. A wave of anticipatory energy flooded the room and the show began, instantly captivating Tash. By the final number, they were standing and clapping along with everyone else, including the older couple next to them.

"That was brilliant," Aidan said as they slowly made their way out.

"I knew from the opening number. Anything that starts with coveting shoes has to be good."

He raised his eyebrows.

"Kidding. I loved it."

When they stepped into the cool night air, Aidan asked, "What now?"

"Come to my place."

They walked to the subway station, still talking about the play.

Aidan said, "What was so beautiful about that was the message of accepting others as they are. So simple."

"Yet so hard," Tash said.

"Especially when we can't accept ourselves as we are. That's the real challenge, right?"

"I guess."

Soon they were back in Tash's bed, making love with their eyes wide open. They never spoke about their relationship, but after that night they became inseparable.

CHAPTER 4

Jason's life was a series of late night see-and-be-seen parties. Suddenly the "it" guy of New York, the city was his playground. He went to club openings, enjoyed backroom VIP treatment at his regular haunts, and was the person every guy and sexually confused girl wanted to take home. His lucrative and exclusive modeling contract made his time his own, other than occasional photo shoots, public appearances, and international trips for fashion shows.

Most days he slept in, ran a few miles, practiced yoga, and hung around the apartment reading until it was time to head out for the night. When Tash had time off, they snuggled in his bed, watching movies or marathons of their favorite talk shows. Sometimes they bummed around the city, shopping and checking out art galleries. When he suspected Tash's credit card bills were out of control, which was most of the time, he'd treat her to new shoes or accessories to discourage her from overspending.

Over the last six weeks, he spent many days hanging out with Aidan, who had basically moved in. Aidan worked at night so they had plenty of time together when Tash was at work during the day. They bonded quickly, sharing a love of *Monty Python*, sarcastic humor, and gently teasing Tash. Aidan was sensitive to Jason and Tash's close relationship; he knew when to pick up food or grab something from his apartment so they could have their alone time.

On this Friday, Jason woke up at seven thirty for a nine o'clock call time. It was his first solo commercial shoot and he stayed in the night before to get a good night's rest. Tash left him a note by the coffee pot that read, "You got this, rock star. XOXO."

Unfortunately, the subway was delayed. He arrived at the soundstage at nine thirty and was rushed into hair styling. After more than half an hour getting his hair to look naturally tousled, he plopped down in his makeup chair.

A short man with dark hair greeted him. "Hi, I'm Sam, and I'll be doing your makeup today."

"Hey," Jason replied, so busy texting that he didn't even look up from his phone.

"We're going to do a matte look today, nothing iridescent for commercial shoots."

"Uh, huh. Whatever, dude," Jason mumbled.

Sam pursed his lips in annoyance at the very moment Jason looked up to see himself in the mirror. Sam blushed, clearly embarrassed.

"I'm sorry I was running late," Jason said.

"The talent is always late."

"There was a problem on the subway. I'm usually on time."

"Uh huh. That's fine. Please turn to your right," Sam replied.

Twenty minutes later, Sam sprayed a finishing shield on Jason's face and said, "You're all set. I'll go see if they're ready."

"Thanks, man."

When Sam returned, he said, "Wardrobe is waiting for you."

Jason stood up, slipped his phone into his pocket, and said, "You know, I'm a little nervous."

"Haven't you done this before?"

"Group shoots. Sometimes I was like the lead, but I've never shot solo."

Sam sneered. "You just have to stand there with your hands in your pockets and gaze off into the distance while a voiceover guy sells cologne. You'll be fine."

Jason was taken aback. It had been a long time since anyone had spoken to him that way. His face revealed his surprise, and Sam looked mortified, his cheeks reddening. Before either broke the silence, a frazzled-looking woman stormed over.

"Come on, come on. Let's get you in some jeans."

Jason followed her, but not without a glance back at Sam.

Throughout the day, Sam retouched Jason's makeup on set. With a crowd of people around, the bright lights burning and cameras rolling, neither said a word. As Jason was leaving the shoot five hours later, Sam ran up to him.

"Listen, I wanted to apologize to you. I didn't mean to be so rude. I'm very sorry."

"No worries, dude. I actually wanted to apologize to you."

"What for?" Sam asked.

"For not seeing you. When I first sat down, I was so preoccupied I didn't really meet you properly. I got us off on the wrong foot. I'm sorry."

"Uh, okay. Wow, uh thanks," Sam said, flustered.

Jason looked confused.

"I'm sorry. I don't mean to be, well, so incoherent. It's just that most people don't surprise me."

"Yeah, me either," Jason said before walking away.

*

"I can't believe you have to spend this long on the subway just to get anywhere. That sucks," Tash said, as the train roared into their stop.

Aidan smiled. "I use it as a chance to read or put my headphones on and get lost in new music. The subway has its own sound too, like the rest of the city. Sometimes I shut my eyes and feel the sound."

"I guess. You have a better attitude than me."

He laughed. "It's all I can afford, and as you'll see, it's not much. It's actually way better than my first crash pad in the city. I never would have brought a girl there, not even once."

"No offense, but I hate the subway. This would drive me nuts," Tash said as they exited the station.

"You do what you have to do. I'd kill for a place like yours. I still don't know how you manage to afford such a sweet place in that neighborhood."

Tash took in the sights and smells of the neighborhood. Many of the buildings were in decline but she admired the vibrant graffiti. Aidan greeted a few guys standing in line at a food truck.

"Who are they?" Tash asked.

"They live in my old building. Nice guys. Met them when I couldn't get my futon up the stairs. They helped. The little guy did some of the subversive street art you were checking out."

"Cool." They continued walking, but moments later Tash complained, "I can't believe you have such a long walk on top of that subway ride."

"We're almost there, beauty queen. The truth is, I would sacrifice anything to be in a major city – Chicago, New York, whatever. I just can't go back to the 'burbs and bullshit."

"Yeah, I still can't picture you in a place like that."

"Neither can I. I'd rather scrape to get by and be here in the middle of it all. Here I can just *be*. I'm not really into material stuff anyway, just people, places, and music. The deejay thing has its benefits too. I never pay cover charges."

"And you don't drink so you go out to the best places for free."

"Exactly."

"Pretty sweet."

"Okay, here we are," he said as he unlocked the door to a dilapidated walk-up.

Tash smiled.

"Don't worry; you don't have to start hanging out here. Thanks for coming with me. I just want to grab some clothes for tonight."

"Sure, but I don't know if I'm up to going to Brooklyn with you tonight. You'll be there late and I need to catch up on some sleep. You know I have to go to the store tomorrow morning."

"No worries. We can go for a bite and I can get you a cab before I head to the subway."

They entered the rancid-smelling building, and Tash followed Aidan to the stairwell. She put her foot on the first stair heading up, but he pulled her hand.

"This way," he said, leading her downstairs.

"You live in the basement?"

"Think of it as the ground floor."

She followed him into the tiny studio apartment, which was about the size of the small common room in her apartment, and she wondered if the bars on the windows made him feel more or less safe.

"Can you believe I have a weekend roommate?" he asked sarcastically.

"Uh no, I literally don't understand how that even works," she said, noticing one couch and no other places to sit.

"It was a bigger problem before I started seeing you. Couldn't swing this place on my own and my friend needed a place to crash on weekends because he's got a part-time job in the city. He pitches in a little rent and it's enough for me to get by. He used to sleep in a sleeping bag on the floor and I'd take the futon."

"Fuck," she said.

"When I have good gigs on the weekends I'm out all night anyway. Do you want a glass of water or something?"

"No thanks," she said, rifling through his shelves. "Wow! I can't believe you have all of these VHS tapes. I mean, that's crazy."

"When I first moved to the city, I went to this charity place to score some furniture and they had a working VCR for five bucks. You can still buy old VHS tapes for like a dollar online and at stores all over the Village, so I figured why not."

"How can you have the most modern laptop, headphones, and deejay setup and be watching freaking VHS tapes?"

"I spend my money on the things that matter. Plus the "be kind, rewind" stickers are hilarious. The retro thing is kind of rad."

"Oh my God, you have *Staying Alive*," she said. "Finola Hughes was so beautiful in this. I remember when Travolta's character, uh…"

"Tony."

"Yeah! He said that watching her dance was like watching smoke move. Brilliant line. Totally captures what lust feels like. But God, the rest of the thing was so cheesy."

"Come on, that was Travolta at his best. The soundtrack was killer for the time too."

She raised her shoulders and continued flipping through movies. "Is this any good?" she asked, holding up a tape.

"*Heathers*? Don't tell me you haven't seen it."

"Nope."

"It's great. Completely dated but great. It's the original *Mean Girls*, only darker. Total cult classic. With your eighties fascination I would have guessed that you knew it by heart."

"Wanna watch?" she asked.

He looked at the clock on the microwave before saying, "Sure. I could run to the takeout truck down the street and pick up dinner. We can watch it before I head to work."

"Cool. I'll wait here."

"What do you want from the truck, beef or chicken?"

"Just get me whatever the veggie option is. I never warmed to the idea of meat from a truck."

He smiled. "Yes, your majesty."

"Hardy har har."

Aidan returned twenty minutes later. The couch was set up with pillows and a blanket, and the small coffee table was cleared to make room for their food. Aidan smiled and said, "I see that my place brings out the domestic goddess in you. Very unexpected."

"Oh please," she said casually.

"Nah, it's cute. You wanted to make things nice. I dig it," he said with a sly smile.

She rolled her eyes and tried to blow him off but was given away by the ever-so-slight upward turn in the corners of her mouth.

While Aidan cracked open the soda cans, Tash opened the food containers and released the smells of the Middle East into the small space. "Oh no, they put peppers on yours," she said.

"Ah, you remembered I don't like 'em. No worries. I'll pick them out."

"I'll get it," she said as she scooped the peppers out of his container and into hers.

"Thanks for looking out for me," he said.

"More for me."

Aidan put the tape in the VCR and said, "The one bad thing about buying this thing used is that it didn't come with a remote. But hey, I'd probably lose it anyway."

"Not in this tiny place," she quipped.

"Touché, beauty queen."

"Wow, this is really good," she said as she took a forkful of her rice and veggie mixture. "Thanks for dinner."

"Sure thing. There's some pita in the bag."

"Cool," she said, reaching for it.

"Okay, so here we go," he said as the opening credits rolled.

Tash placed her food container on her lap and leaned into Aidan's shoulder. As the movie began, she nestled into him, her eyes lit up, and she declared, "Oh my God. The colors are brilliant."

CHAPTER 5

As Tash spooned coffee grounds into the filter, Jason crept into the doorway and said, "You're up early."

She dumped the grounds all over the kitchen counter. "Jeez, you startled me," she said.

"Sorry."

"Do you want some coffee?" she asked as she wiped the grounds into the palm of her hand and threw them in the kitchen sink.

Jason shook his head. "No thanks. I'm going to try to catch a yoga class. Why are you up so early on a Saturday, and where's Aidan?"

"He was spinning at a club in Brooklyn last night. I was too beat to go and didn't want him to wake me up at like four in the morning, so he crashed at his place. Oh my God, I went to his place yesterday."

"Well it's about time."

"Oh, shut up."

"He said it's tiny. Is it awful?"

"Yeah, it's pretty heinous but we had a good time. He has an old VCR and all of these great movies. We watched *Heathers,* which was totally disturbed."

"Never saw it."

"See, he thought I was a freak for not seeing it before. I'll have to tell him that you've never seen it either."

"Well you are the movie maven."

"True. Anyway, I needed sleep last night. I have to go into the store for a couple of hours to deal with a shipment; Isabelle has a callback. He's meeting me there and then we're going out for a bite with Kyle."

"Ooooh, that's big! Introducing him to the one relative you actually like. What's next, a little walk down the aisle?"

"Oh shut up," she said with a roll of her eyes. "It's just lunch, drama queen."

Jason smiled. "You know I think Aidan is the bomb. I'm just teasing you."

Tash opened the cabinets in search of a travel mug. "So, rock star, how did your shoot go yesterday? And why weren't you out partying all night?"

"Um, it was okay."

"Uh, hold up," she said, giving her full attention to Jason. "Just okay? What happened?"

"It was fine. It's just that I was late because of a problem on the damn subway and some guy sort of said something to me about it."

"Who?" Tash asked.

"The makeup guy, Sam."

"Who gives a shit what the makeup guy said? He was probably jealous of you. I bet you could have gotten him in trouble."

"It wasn't like that. It was more of a misunderstanding. I was kind of rude to him but I didn't mean to be."

"So I think the pressing question is: why are you still thinking about this? Who cares?"

Jason didn't respond.

As she poured her coffee, Tash pronounced, "Ooooh, I seeeeee. This is about a boy. Shall we call him Makeup Boy? Will you be going down the Clinique aisle? Or going down …."

"Ha, ha, ha. Very funny. It's not like that at all. If you had seen this guy, you wouldn't be saying that. He was *so* not my type."

"Say what you want, but you're the one still talking about Makeup Boy." Tash grabbed her coffee and breezed past Jason, stopping to kiss him on the cheek. "Have fun at yoga," she whispered.

*

Tash looked up from the large cardboard box she was unpacking and noticed Aidan wandering around the store.

"Aidan, come here and help," she called from the door of the backroom.

"Hey, babe. Love the space of this store. The whole purple and black thing against the glossy cherry wood floors is badass."

"Hey. Hold this open," Tash said, handing him a large garbage bag.

Aidan sat on a small stool and held the bag as Tash stuffed it full of discarded styrofoam packing materials. "Why do they pack the shipments in this non-recyclable crap?" Aidan asked. "It's so retro, and not in a good way."

Tash sat on the floor, collecting errant Styrofoam bits. She looked up at him, clearly annoyed. "Think I know? Let's just finish so we can get the hell out of here. What time is it, anyway?"

Aidan looked at his phone. "Twelve fifteen."

"Shit, we're late. Let me just go to the bathroom," she said, tossing the full garbage bag aside.

They finished up at the store and headed to Café Borgia. The little SoHo staple was busting at the seams. Tash spotted her cousin sitting in the far right-hand corner. She slid into the booth next to Kyle, and Aidan took the opposite seat.

"I'm so sorry we're late," she said as she leaned over and hugged him.

He laughed. "I would expect nothing less. I know how you like to make a grand entrance."

"That's why it sucks; I was planning to be on time for once, but I got held up at work."

"It's good to know some things haven't changed."

She rolled her eyes. Noticing Aidan sitting there silently smiling, she said, "Oh sorry, Aidan, this troublemaker is my little cousin, Kyle."

"As usual, Tash forgot *she's* the troublemaker," Kyle said as he extended his hand.

"Nice to meet you," Aidan said, still smiling.

"What's so amusing ?" Tash asked.

"It's just fun to see someone else mocking you. Plus I think it's adorable that you always seem surprised you're late," Aidan said.

"I like this guy already," Kyle said as Tash shook her head.

They all laughed. A moment later, the waitress came over to take their lunch orders.

"The ham and cheese sandwich and a coffee, please," Kyle said.

"And for you?" the waitress asked Tash.

"A slice of today's quiche with salad and coffee, please."

"Same for me," Aidan said.

"It's not the same as the blintzes, is it?" Kyle asked Tash.

She shook her head.

"What's that?" Aidan asked.

"There's a diner Kyle and I go to. We always share a platter of cheese blueberry blintzes. They're outrageous. The coffee sucks, but they give you a plate of bagel chips and stuff while you're waiting."

"Except Tash eats the nasty cinnamon raisin bagel chips."

"I like them. Shut up."

Aidan smiled. "So, are you ever gonna take me for blintzes?"

"I don't know. We'll see," she said coyly.

After some small talk, their food was served. Kyle and Aidan scarfed theirs down. Tash teased them, saying, "What is it about guys and food? I mean, breathe!" While Tash leisurely nibbled on her meal, Aidan filled Kyle in on how they met. Tash interjected from time to time, insisting that Aidan was "infatuated the second he saw me." They talked about Kyle's life as a political science major at Columbia. When Aidan asked if he was seeing anyone, Tash proceeded to give him unsolicited dating advice. "Listen you, with those freaky exes; you are so not giving me advice." Aidan jumped in and insisted that he dish on her past beaus, and soon they were both teasing her mercilessly. Tash shook her head and smiled, giving in to the absurdity of it all.

When the laughter died down, the conversation moved to shared interests in music and movies.

An hour later, they all threw down some cash and Aidan excused himself to use the restroom. With only a one-person unisex restroom available, they saw Aidan waiting in line across the café and knew they had a little time alone.

Tash opened her mouth, but before she could say anything, Kyle said, "Aidan is great."

She was surprised. "You never like the guys I date."

"First of all, they've hardly been guys – more like trolls," he said with a laugh.

She playfully punched his arm.

"None of the guys you've dated have been even remotely good enough for you. You deserve someone who gets you."

She smiled.

"Anyway, he's great. So here's hoping he doesn't dump you," he said as he burst into hysterics.

"Hey!" she said, again punching him in the arm. "You know me – I don't take things too seriously anyway."

"Maybe you should this time. What does Jason think of him?"

"He's in love with Aidan, but in a brother kind of way. You should see them together."

"Maybe Aidan is the roommate he always wanted," Kyle said through laughter.

"Hey! I'm gonna punch you harder next time."

"Okay, I surrender," he said, putting his hands up. "But seriously, if Jason and I both think he's good for you, maybe you should lean into it a bit."

"Let's worry about getting you a date before worrying about my boyfriend."

"Oh my God, you called him your boyfriend!"

"That's it, smarty," she said as she walloped him.

"Okay, okay, I'm moving on. How are your folks?"

"Fine I guess. I haven't visited in a while. What about yours?"

"Um, I guess they're all right."

"What is it Kye?"

"Probably nothing. They just seem, I don't know, like something's up."

"Well, didn't your mom start a new job as an agent or something? She's probably just really busy."

"Yeah, maybe. Anyway, they're fine. What about Jason, is his star still rising?"

Aidan returned and sat back down, not wanting to interrupt.

"He just had his first shoot as a solo model in a commercial. It's freaking crazy. I'm so happy for him. And I think he met a boy, although he says he didn't."

"When does he not have a new dude on his arm? That guy has game," Aidan chimed in.

"Don't say anything to him. It might be nothing and I don't want him to be mad at me."

"What about Penelope, how's she?" Kyle asked.

"She's had a low profile lately, hardly ever home. No annoying notes."

"Low profile? I'd say more like downright mysterious," Aidan said. "I've probably seen her two or three times and I've barely left your place for weeks."

"She must be there more often than that," Tash said.

Aidan shrugged.

"Is she dating someone?" Kyle asked.

"I doubt it. I think she's just really busy with school and she visits her dad a lot and stuff. She's most likely spending her nights curled up to a library book. You know, the dusty, big-word kind she likes so much."

"You used to be good friends."

"Yeah, that was before we lived together."

"You lived together in college."

"I was abroad like for half of that year. She didn't have enough time to get on my nerves."

"She's a sweetheart; you should be nicer to her. Grad school is probably stressful, too," Kyle said.

"You see sweet, I see uptight," Tash said.

Kyle shot her a stern look.

"Yeah, yeah, yeah. I'll make an effort. Okay gentleman, ready to go?"

They left the café, hugging each other on the street outside before Kyle took off in one direction and Tash and Aidan in the other.

*

Tash and Aidan spent the next few hours wandering from SoHo back to the Village. They looked in store windows and stopped in art galleries.

"Come here," she said, pulling him into a gallery featuring Andy Warhol prints.

"Warhol was ahead of his time," Aidan said as they walked through the gallery.

"I know. Can you imagine what he would say about reality television?"

"He predicted it. I don't think he'd be surprised in the least," Aidan said.

"Uh huh. I love the Marilyns," she said, stopping in front of one of Warhol's most iconic pieces.

"Of course you do, beauty queen."

"Shut up," she said, playfully punching his arm. "I saw a documentary about her in college. Did you know when she talked to reporters she used to say, 'Would you like me to be her for you?' or something like that. She knew Marilyn was a character she created."

"Or one side of her personality," Aidan suggested.

"Exactly. It was like she was able to hold on to both Norma and Marilyn."

"But kind of fucked up if she never integrated them, right? I mean, living as two people instead of one whole person can't be easy. Maybe that's why she…"

"Oh don't even say it. I never believed she killed herself."

He smiled. "Neither did I, but that doesn't mean she was happy."

Tash shrugged.

"That's what was so brilliant about Warhol. He captured the lie and shoved it in everyone's face, decorated in bright, psychotically happy colors."

"Can I tell you something?" she asked, turning toward him.

"Of course."

"You know how some people have this romantic notion of New York in the 1920s?"

"Uh, rich white people might."

"Shut up," she said, punching his arm harder this time.

"I'm just kidding. Yeah, I know what you're talking about. People who read a lot of Edith Wharton or whatever."

"Well, I have this romantic notion of New York in the 1980s. I think that's why I've been so obsessed with the films lately. My medium has always been film; it's how I connect with different times and ideas."

Aidan smiled. "You always light up when you talk about film."

She shrugged. "Anyway, I have this love of New York in the 1980s, you know when the Mary Boone Gallery was the hottest place in SoHo, not a freaking H&M or whatever. The time of Warhol and all of those pop visionaries."

"You know who I love from back then? Basquiat. Nobody blurred graffiti and art like that before he did. He was exposing the lie too, I think, but in his own way. I think the bullshit is really what killed him."

"Totally. I'm telling you, when Mary Boone closed her SoHo gallery and opened on Fifth Avenue, something died forever."

They smiled at each other and finished their tour of the gallery.

Once outside, Tash bought a black fedora from a street vendor. "How do I look?"

"Too cool for school, beauty queen."

"You're so lame," she teased, before grabbing his hand and continuing their stroll.

They were a few blocks from Tash's apartment when Aidan received a text message.

"Hey, a couple of my friends are in the neighborhood and they invited us for a drink. You up for it?"

"Sure."

A few minutes later, they sat down on the patio of a local Italian restaurant with Aidan's friends Jaime and Stu, both of whom Tash liked instantly. Jaime's black hair, black sundress, combat boots, and row of silver-studded earrings gave her a gothic look. Tash knew her appearance was just one facet of her personality when she greeted them ironically with, "Hello, happy shiny people." Jaime grabbed Aidan's arm. "Did you see the cover of *The Economist*, with the belly flop? Hysterical. Reminded me of what you said about Republicans." Not only did her outgoing personality contrast her gothic look, but Tash suspected she was wickedly smart. *I like her*, she thought. Tash pegged her as late twenties, maybe early thirties.

"Jaime works as a satirist for an art and culture magazine and freelances on the side, so we're always talking about art and politics," Aidan said, filling Tash in. "She got her master's in journalism at NYU, actually."

"Oh, Jaime, there's something on that seat. Let me get a napkin for you," Stu said as he raised his hand to get the attention of a waiter.

He's a sweetheart. And God, he's even taller than Aidan. He could be a basketball player, Tash thought.

"Stu works as a personal assistant, so he's used to taking care of people," Jaime said.

"Who do you work for?" Tash asked Stu as he wiped Jaime's seat.

"I work for a New York celebrity," he said.

"But due to a confidentiality agreement, he's not allowed to reveal any details," Jaime added.

Tash's eyes lit up.

"Oh, don't be impressed," Jaime said. "He's basically a manservant."

Stu winced. "I can't even disagree. It's true. It's sad and true."

"You guys seem like an old married couple," Tash said.

"Oh he wishes, but we're just roommates," Jaime said.

"Yeah, if only she had a penis," Stu said.

"And if only you had boobs!" Jaime added. They all dissolved in a fit of laughter.

Tash fit in as if she'd known them for years. Before long, they were on their second carafe of the house red, sharing fried calamari and a bread basket. Aidan couldn't stop smiling, and Tash was having a great time.

Jaime said, "So Tash, Aidan tells me you studied film at NYU."

"Yup."

"Did you ever have Professor Mercer?"

"Oh, I totally did. I signed up for some semiotics class, having no idea what it was. God, that was so boring."

"I took a class with him too; it was awful. It sucked because it was the only class I took in the film department but I didn't realize what it really was either. It killed my elective space."

"Did you like NYU?" Tash asked.

"Loved it. Of course, I'll still be paying off my student loans when I'm in the retirement home. I love my job but my salary is truly pathetic. That's why I have to share a place with this one," she said smirking at Stu. "What about you? Did you like NYU?"

"Yeah. I partied too much the first couple of years, so my folks didn't get their money's worth. Once I settled in, I loved the classes for my major. I'm really into avant-garde film studies and there were some amazing professors. I was constantly going to hear speakers outside of class and going to film screenings, especially senior year. You know, all the perks that aren't for your grade. I just loved it all and couldn't get enough."

"You should think about going to grad school and doing something with it."

"I thought about going for an MFA in cinematography. Maybe. I don't know if I could do the school schedule thing again."

Aidan chimed in, "I know you could do it and I think it would be awesome for you. You have an amazing eye and it's obviously your passion."

She shrugged and changed the conversation.

Before they left, Tash and Jaime went to the ladies room together.

"It's so great to finally you meet you," Jaime said as they fixed their lipstick.

"You too."

"He talks about you all the time."

"Really?"

"Oh yeah. He won't shut up about you. He told us he met a beautiful girl who was smart as hell, and that we'd like her because she doesn't let him get away with anything."

Tash smiled.

Soon they were all standing in the street, saying their goodbyes and making plans to attend an animated short film festival the following month. Aidan took Tash's hand and they headed in the direction of her apartment.

"Your friends are pretty cool," Tash said.

He squeezed her hand. "Yeah, they're good eggs."

She giggled.

"They're sharp too. You know, Jaime was on point. You should do something in film. Is it a money thing, not going to grad school?"

"No, my parents can pay to send me."

"Damn. You're so lucky."

"I guess," she said dismissively.

As they approached Washington Square Park, Tash noticed Harold sitting on his favorite bench. A man walking past him flicked a cigarette butt, nearly hitting Harold's foot. *Jackass*, she thought.

"Follow me," she said, leading Aidan over. "Hey there, Harold."

"Hello, Natashya. Isn't dusk extraordinary tonight?"

Tash smiled. "Harold, this is Aidan."

Aidan put his hand out and Harold nodded, sparing him the physical contact. "Nice to meet you, young man. I've noticed you around."

Tash looked at Aidan, "Harold is my buddy. Sometimes we have coffee together in the mornings."

Aidan smiled.

"We gotta go, but I'll try to bring donuts on Monday if it's not raining."

"That would be lovely."

"Goodnight," Tash said.

"Nice to meet you," Aidan said.

Harold tilted his head down and blinked his eyes tightly.

As they walked away, Aidan said, "So what's his deal?"

"I don't know his story. Told him he didn't have to tell me. He's just my friend, sort of. I don't like people mistreating him. Sometimes I bring him coffee and stuff on my way to work. That's all."

Aidan stopped in his tracks, looked Tash in the eyes, and said, "I love you."

"Don't be so dramatic," she blithely said.

"I love you, beauty queen. You know I do."

She smiled. "Let's get out of here, you big sap."

He took her hand and they headed down the street.

*

After washing her face and slipping into an oversized t-shirt, Tash jumped on the bed next to Aidan, who was reading a novel.

"Uh, well hello there, beautiful."

"Listen, it's no big deal or anything, but do you want to see my final film project from college? It's experimental and I couldn't really achieve what I wanted to, but…"

"I would absolutely love to see it," he said softly.

Aidan beamed and Tash fidgeted as they watched it on her laptop. At one point Aidan said, "I love what you did there, with the swirling colors."

"Thanks. See, I had this idea that since cinematography is basically defined as painting with light, that I would mirror that here. I couldn't fully realize the idea, but…"

"But I totally see where you were going. I can actually hear it, like music."

She smiled.

When the short film was over, Aidan said, "You're talented. Truly. I'm so impressed."

"It's kind of my thing I guess. It's the only thing I've ever really been into," she said as she put her laptop away.

"What's your vision? I mean, if you could create something in the film world, what would it be?"

"I always wanted to bring the true pop art sensibility to contemporary film, but not in a cheesy or expected way. You know, something fresh and cutting edge."

He nodded. "Come here."

He put his arm out and pulled her to him. He wrapped his arms around her and whispered, "Thank you for sharing that with me."

She had never felt so close to anyone, and just for a moment, she leaned into the feeling and his embrace.

*

The next morning, Aidan was pouring some orange juice when Penelope came into the kitchen.

"Oh, hey," Aidan said.

"Hi," she said as she set the coffee pot.

"I finally get to see the invisible roommate," Aidan said jokingly.

"I'm not that exciting I guess. Not like Tash and Jason."

"Not at all. I didn't mean it that way. You're just out a lot."

Penelope continued tinkering with the coffee pot.

"I hope you don't mind that I'm here so much," Aidan said.

She shook her head.

"Tash said that you're in graduate school. What are you studying?"

"Art history."

"Oh, wow. Cool. Is that how you and Tash became friends?"

"Uh huh. I think she would say that even in art, she's all about the beautiful and fun parts. I like the boring history. Someone has to, I guess. It's not exciting to most people." Before he could respond, Penelope said, "I'm going to get ready while the coffee is brewing."

"Oh, sure," Aidan said.

She stopped and turned around. "I forgot to let Tash know the monthly bills are on the mail table. I broke everything down so she can just leave me a check. Would you please let her know?"

"Sure."

Tash was busy trying on possible outfits for the day when Aidan returned with two glasses of juice.

"Hey, what do you think of this?" Tash asked as she spun around causing the fringe running down the seams of her white shirt to sway.

"Cute. Very *Urban Cowboy*," he said as he plopped down on her bed. "Oh, before I forget, Penelope said she left your bills on the mail table."

"You talked to her about the bills?"

"All she said was that she divided them up."

"Oh," Tash said as she searched her drawer for matching socks.

"It's kinda nice that she takes care of the accounting stuff for you guys."

"Yeah. She lives for that stuff."

"I still don't know how you can afford this place."

Tash, now more serious, turned to face him. "Jason and Pen pay more than I do. Obviously Jason can afford it and Pen has money from her family. I'm not a mooch. I pay, just less than them."

"That's cool. I didn't mean to make you feel bad. I guess I'm two for two and it's not even noon."

"What?" Tash asked.

"I think I kind of put my foot in my mouth with Penelope."

"Whatever. Don't stress. She's hard to talk to these days."

"Maybe the universe is telling me to close my mouth today. Come here, beauty queen."

"No way. I just got ready and you'll mess me up."

"You're such a girl."

"Yeah, I am."

"Come on," he said. "Just come sit with me. I won't mess you up."

Tash pursed her lips and conceded. Aidan put his hands out, and when she leaned in to take them, he pulled her down, flipped her onto her back, and started tickling her.

"I knew you would mess me up," she squealed through laughter.

He stopped tickling her, brushed her hair from her forehead, and said, "Nothing could mess you up. To me, you are extraordinary."

He kissed her gently. All the while her mind was haunted by a single thought: *You don't really know me.*

PART TWO

CHAPTER 6

Penelope Waters was born in Boston. Her father, Ted, came from an affluent family with deep New England roots and became a corporate attorney because "it was expected." Her mother, Mallory, held a bachelor's degree in finance from Harvard, but pursued a career as a pastry chef because, "Living life means following your dreams." As a child, Penelope was overjoyed to see her mother on the cover of *Boston Magazine*, noted as the most revered pastry chef in the area.

Penelope inherited her father's gravitas. Both were reserved, studious, and above all, serious. Mallory was the opposite. For instance, when she whipped up Penelope's favorite cream puffs, she glazed the tops and smooshed them in rainbow sprinkles.

"Mom, aren't cream puffs supposed to be plain?" Penelope asked.

"There is no such thing as 'supposed to be.' Besides, everything is better covered in sprinkles," she replied.

"Dad, she's being silly again," Penelope complained.

Ted smiled. "She can't help it. Her spirit is as light and airy as those little pastry clouds," he said before popping one in his mouth.

When Penelope spent too much time hunched over her desk, Mallory barged into her room and dragged her outside to look up at the stars. She didn't let her return to her studies until, with pinky fingers hooked, they made a wish together. Secretly, Penelope wished to be more like her mother; despite her ambivalence about "frills," she always kept her hair in long brown spirals, like Mallory's.

When Penelope was seventeen years old, her mother was killed in a car crash. She died instantly, as did the driver responsible, who had been texting. The lightness left their house that day. Although she and her father believed Mallory was in heaven, their shoulders permanently slumped and they never once looked up at the stars.

At Penelope's high school graduation, her father told her that he'd quit his job, sold their Beacon Hill brownstone, and was moving to Vermont to open a bed and breakfast. *He's given up on life*, Penelope thought. While packing her room, half in boxes for storage and half bags for NYU, she was overcome by waves of guilt. *How can I abandon my dad? He seems irreparably damaged.* As guilt shook her confidence in her decision to forge her own path, she found the old *Boston Magazine* with her mother on the cover and remembered how Mallory always encouraged her to be braver and to find herself. *I need to be more like my mother, more fearless.* Mustering all her strength, she lifted herself from the gravity of grief and headed to New York City.

With a major in art history and minor in French, she excelled academically, but was less successful socially. During the first few weeks of freshman year, almost everyone left their doors wide open, popping into each other's rooms, jumping on each other's beds, and quickly forming friendships to carry them through their college years. Grief-stricken and out of her comfort zone, Penelope smiled politely as she walked through the dormitory corridors, but rarely spoke to anyone other than an occasional "excuse me" as she passed groups of friends overtaking the narrow space.

Her roommate was from New York. She spent most nights in her boyfriend's room, also an NYU student, and weekends at home, leaving Penelope on her own. When she saw groups of friends crammed in someone's room, laughing loudly, she wished she could start over again. She berated herself over the time a few girls invited her into their room for a horror movie marathon. With an assignment due the next day, she had hesitated. One girl said, "Don't worry if it's not your thing," and all Penelope could do was smile and walk away. *What's wrong with me?* she wondered as she walked back to her empty dorm room, closing and locking the door behind her as usual.

During her junior year, she took an elective in French cinema. Each Thursday night, students were required to attend a film screening. One night, at a screening of *Betty Blue*, Penelope noticed Tash arriving ten minutes late. As Tash scanned the dark room for an empty seat, Penelope moved over, gesturing for her take the aisle seat.

"Thanks," Tash whispered.

Penelope smiled. "Do you want me to fill you in?" she whispered back.

"Nah, it's one of my favorite movies."

At the end of the screening, Tash turned to Penelope. "So, what did you think?"

"The score was beautiful."

"Is that all?"

"Betty was so self-destructive. Do you think they ever had a chance?" Penelope asked.

"No one in love has a chance," she said with a smirk.

Penelope looked at her blankly.

"I mean, we're each alone, right?" Tash added. "The love illusion just makes people lose their shit." As Penelope wondered if that was true, Tash followed up with, "I'm meeting some friends for a drink. Do you want to come?"

"Oh, it's already pretty late and…"

"You can't be that lame. Come on, live a little."

Remembering the price of hesitation, she responded, "Okay. Just for a little while."

Once at Jelly Belly, a local bar, Tash introduced Pen to a group of girlfriends who were busy rating all the guys in the bar. Penelope sipped a soda while the others slammed the bar's famous Jell-O shots. Supporting a staggering Tash, Penelope got back to her dorm at three in the morning and she didn't care. When Tash slurred, "Thanks. I should really party less and do more of the school thing," Penelope thought, *And I should do the opposite.* They became fast friends, sharing class notes, attending film screenings together, and offering each other honest advice. Penelope became Tash's excuse when she wanted to forgo the party scene for a quiet night in, and Tash became Penelope's passport to the American college experience she had only seen in movies. They roomed together senior year.

One night, Tash met Jason at a club when she was having trouble getting in.

"Screw you! I'm on the damn list. Maybe you should look again," she was yelling at the bouncer. Out of the blue, with a wink from Jason, she was in.

"Thanks! My friend was supposed to get me on the list but I guess she fucked up," she said once they were inside.

He smiled. "No sweat. You're gorgeous – you would have better luck flirting than screaming."

"Yeah, I tried that. Asshole said he had a girlfriend. Like I care. I just wanted to get in."

Jason laughed.

"So, you're pretty connected to just waltz in here like that," she said with a coy smile.

"Honey, I don't play for your team. But nice work with the flirting. I totally want to buy you a drink."

They loved each other immediately. Tash introduced Jason and Penelope and they all became friends. When Tash was getting ready to graduate, she and Jason made a plan to live together.

"Come on, Pen, move in with us," Tash cajoled.

"Yeah, we need a grown-up," Jason added.

"Grad school is going to be hard. I'll need a quiet place to study and I don't want to cramp your style."

"We need you, Pen. Don't worry, we'll behave," Tash said.

At first, the three spent a lot of time together hanging out in their apartment, watching movies or reality show marathons. They all squeezed onto Jason's bed with Tash in the middle, and laughed for hours at corny rom-coms. Tash threw her arms up and melodramatically reenacted the ridiculous "you're the one" speeches, as she called them. Jason mused that if they only had more gay storylines, it wouldn't be so cliché. Then he and Tash stood up, created new characters, and played out the climax scene. They didn't stop until Penelope's giggle morphed into a hearty laugh. Over time, such instances were fewer and farther between. As Jason's star rose, he spent more time going to clubs. Tash loved tagging along, but Penelope studied during the week and often traveled to Vermont on weekends. Tash and Jason's bond grew and Penelope felt increasingly lonely.

By the end of their second year in the apartment, Jason was famous throughout the city, Tash was spending every free moment with Aidan, and Penelope was quietly trying to finish graduate school.

Having completed her last semester of classes, Penelope planned to use the summer to finish her thesis. She had uncharacteristically fallen behind. She claimed to have gotten held up trying to pick the perfect topic, something intellectually interesting that her committee would approve. Everyone accepted this excuse as it affirmed their assumptions about her. The truth was something no one would expect.

*

I'll deal with it today, once and for all, Penelope thought as she stared in the bathroom mirror, searching for herself. *This can't continue. I wasn't thinking. I have to get out before anyone gets hurt. How could things get so complicated?*

She finished getting ready and jammed a few overdue library books into her backpack. Noticing the cover of one book about the Greek goddesses, she wondered, *Why did I pick this of all topics for my thesis? I miss being smart.*

Tash and Jason were cuddling on his bed as she passed his bedroom. Without meaning to, she stopped outside the partially open door and listened.

"Meet us there at ten. There's a bigwig club promoter coming to meet with Aidan and he needs good energy."

"You're relentless. I told you I should stay in tonight. We're shooting at a bunch of outdoor locations tomorrow and there's an early call time."

"Sleep during the day and just come for one drink. I'm not relentless, I'm restless. It's not just Aidan, I need you there. He's being really clingy and I need a…"

"You don't need me. He's not clingy, T. Come on, what gives?"

"His 'I love you' stuff freaks me out. What does he even know about me?"

"He knows what matters. Stop letting the past mess with your head."

"What if…"

Penelope caught herself eavesdropping and quickly scampered out of the apartment. The warm air caressed her face as she stepped onto the street. *It's a beautiful day. Too bad I'll be stuck inside.*

Soon she was at her regular haunt, the library, where she planned to spend the day working on her thesis. As soon as she sat down and opened her laptop, her phone beeped with an incoming text.

`Meet me?`

After inhaling slowly, she responded.

`Tonight. At the library now. Need to concentrate on work.`

She slipped her phone into her backpack and started reading. Stopping only once to go next door for a veggie wrap and smoothie, Penelope worked all day, taking such copious notes that her fingers hurt from typing. While her thesis focused on representations of Persephone, she became increasingly tired and began running searches on some of the other Greek goddesses. An amateur blog about Penelope, her namesake, captured her attention. The blogger described Penelope as faithful and loyal, suggesting she not only married a hero, but was herself a hero. It was no wonder she was her father's favorite. *That's it. I can't take it anymore. My dad would be so disappointed.*

As she switched her computer off, a librarian passed by. "Can I return those books to the stacks for you?"

"Yes, thank you," she said. She pulled her phone out of her bag and sent a text.

Leaving the library now. Meet me.

The response was almost instantaneous.

On my way.

The library seemed to stop time, concealing the day from the night. By the time she left, the sky was dark. *I wonder if Tash convinced Jason to go out with her. They always have so much fun.* She hailed a cab and was on her way, with all of her thoughts redirected to the impossible task ahead.

As the driver pulled up to The Plaza, she remembered the first time she saw it. *Just like in the movies*, she thought. Although not materialistic or interested in the city's ever-changing hotspots, this New York landmark had once taken on a mythic quality in her imagination. She could still hear her mother reading the *Eloise* books to her, and their family movie nights often featured scenes at The Plaza. Suddenly feeling ashamed for having denigrated her childhood memories, she climbed out of the cab and marched into the hotel with conviction. *I will end it.*

*

Tash arrived at the club at ten thirty, half an hour late to meet Aidan who was already waiting inside. Wearing a sparkling black mini-dress and matching high heels, she looked like a movie star. Her hair was pimped out in perfect loose curls and her severe makeup was capped off with cherry red lipstick. Her style was all at once soft and hard, just like the dreamy trip-hop music swirling in the industrial club.

She made her way through the large industrial space featuring exposed pipes contrasted with a perimeter of lush black leather sofas. The blaring trip-hop music and soft blue lighting around the bars set the mood. As she scanned the room both for

Aidan and random celebrities, a tall, dark-haired guy dressed head to toe in Gucci offered to buy her a drink. Before she could respond, Aidan was beside her.

"Another time," she said to the guy as she turned to Aidan.

"Fending off your suitors already? Not surprised. You look amazing," he said.

"Well, that'll teach you not to wait for me outside."

"This place is pretty sick, isn't it?"

Tash nodded. "I guess. It's kind of nineties wannabe."

"The music is pretty sexy. And see that roped off area over there?" he said, pointing to a mezzanine level.

"Uh huh."

"That's the VIP area. We have a private table waiting for when Tony and his crew arrive. It's pretty sweet."

"Not bad," she conceded.

"I heard there are some reality stars hanging around, so that should make it worth your while."

"Really? Who's here?"

Aidan laughed. "Don't know. But when you see them you can tell me all about it."

"Okay, smartie. How about you buy me a drink already?"

After a strong cocktail and half an hour of dancing, Tash pulled Aidan close to her and said, "I have to go to the bathroom."

"Sure. I'm going to wait at the table. Tony should be here any minute. Meet me there. You're on the list."

He leaned in to kiss her on the cheek, but she pulled away too quickly.

This is tacky, Tash thought as she entered one of the unisex bathrooms. After relieving herself, she waited for a sink and mirror.

"Damn girl, you're hot," said a young guy who reeked of beer.

When she raised her eyebrow in response, he adopted a more hostile tone. "Can't you take a compliment?"

She turned to face him and said, "Thank you. All right?"

"You don't have to be a bitch. You're not all that, you just look easy. Thought you might do me in a stall. Fucking cunt," he said before stumbling out of the restroom.

"That guy's just a dick," a nearby woman said. "Don't let him get to you. Girls have been turning him down all night and he's not taking it well."

"Thanks," Tash said as she slipped her lipstick into her purse.

As she turned to walk away, the woman called after her. "Hey, come here."

"Yeah?"

The woman pulled a tiny plastic bag filled with white powder out of her Jimmy Choo clutch. "Do you need something to take the edge off?"

Tash stared at the little bag. At first, she was offended. *What the hell? Do I give off junky whore vibes?* But her outrage morphed into temptation. As she contemplated her choices, the woman pulled out another little bag.

"I also have some X if that's more your thing."

A chill went up her spine. Flashes of a horrible night from years earlier surfaced – she had woken up in a boyfriend's bed with him and his roommate, fearing what happened to her while she was unconscious.

"I haven't done that shit since college and I don't plan to start again," she said firmly before leaving the bathroom.

Despite her swagger, she was rattled. She leaned against a wall for a moment before heading to the bar and downing a shot of tequila to calm her nerves.

By the time she got up to the VIP section, Aidan was having an intense conversation with a group of people. When he didn't notice her approaching the table, her mind spiraled. *Fucking great. Maybe if he were a gentleman he would have met me downstairs. Now I have to chat it up with these tools. Can't believe Jason didn't even come. If...*

Her thoughts trailed off as Aidan saw her and waved her over, scooting over on the semi-circle leather couch to make room for her.

"Everyone, this is my girlfriend, Tash," he said.

Everyone smiled and nodded. The man directly across from her extended his hand and said, "I'm Tony. Nice to meet you."

"You too," she said.

As the group conversation resumed, Aidan whispered in her ear, "You were gone a while. I was getting worried you ditched me."

"I was dealing with a douchebag in the gross unisex bathroom."

"What happened?"

"Maybe if you had come with me you would know." Aidan looked stunned. Tash said, "Whatever, don't worry about it. It's not a big deal."

Tony redirected Aidan's attention. "Aidan, tell me more about your ideas for themed party nights."

Aidan squeezed Tash's hand and resumed his conversation with Tony. A few minutes later, the waitress stopped by. Tash ordered a shot of tequila, which she slammed back the second it was served.

As the night progressed, Tash became increasingly bored listening to Aidan talk music with Tony and his entourage. Despite his promises, there were only a couple of D-list pseudo-celebrities there, but none of them interested her. Desperate to shake things up, she coyly looked over at Tony and gave him a half smile, catching his attention.

"Aidan, I think your lovely girlfriend might like to dance."

"Oh," Aidan said, jarred. "I'm sorry Tash, are you fed up with music talk?"

"No, but I would like to dance," she said as she stood up.

Aidan started to slide toward the edge of the booth, but Tash looked at Tony, extended her arm, and said, "Shall we?"

"Well, how could I resist such a beautiful woman? Aidan, you don't mind do you?"

"No, man," he said, clearly dumbfounded.

Aidan watched as Tash and Tony walked down to the main dance floor, where she led him to the center stage, pulled him close to her, and danced seductively with him for nearly half an hour to Hooverphonic remixes. She was so tipsy that he had to hold her up a few times but she refused to return to the booth. Aidan watched from the mezzanine. When they came back to the table, Aidan jumped up and said, "I think I should probably get Tash home."

"I think Tash can decide when Tash should go home," she slurred.

"Are we good, Tony? Can we follow up by email?"

Tony nodded.

"See you, man," Aidan said as he took Tash's hand to leave.

When they reached the front door of the club, she pushed his hand aside and said, "I don't like being manhandled."

"What the hell is your problem?"

"I don't have a problem."

"The one time I need you to do something for me so that I can make a good impression and land a job, you get wasted and flirt with the club promoter? Are you kidding me?"

"This is just who I am."

"No, it's who you're afraid people think you are."

"Leave it alone," Tash mumbled.

"It or you?"

"Same difference."

"No, it's not the same. What is *it* anyway? What's wrong with you? Just tell me," Aidan pleaded.

"I'm getting a cab. You can come with me or not," she said as she tottered outside.

"I want to make sure you get home safely," Aidan said.

Neither said a word in the cab. At one point Tash thought he was going to say something so she opened her window and stuck her face into the breeze.

When they got to her apartment, Tash walked in but Aidan stood outside the door.

"Are you coming in or not?" she asked in an irritated tone.

"I don't know. We need to talk but I think you should sleep it off first."

"I'm not drunk."

"Yeah, right."

"We can't talk here. Jason is probably sleeping. He has a big day tomorrow. Come to my room."

Aidan followed Tash in, locking the door behind them. When they got to her bedroom, she sat on her bed to take her shoes off. Aidan leaned against the bedroom door, arms crossed.

In a quiet and calm voice he asked, "What was that tonight, with Tony? Why did you do that?"

She shrugged. "I was bored."

"You were bored? Big freaking deal. You weren't the center of attention for all of five minutes, but that doesn't mean you have to go crazy. You're so damn narcissistic, but it's all bullshit. There's more to you behind this wall of crap."

She didn't respond.

"Fuck, that's it. I can't take it anymore," he said, wringing his hands.

"Then leave."

"Don't you get it? I don't want to leave. I want to be with you but you need to confront your stuff."

"I'm not your fucking project."

"Everyone has stuff to deal with. Stop pretending. Let me in."

"I'm fine the way I am."

"Really? Let's examine things. You went to NYU to study film, which you're passionate about, but you work as a part-time sales clerk instead. Do you know how many friends I have that pounded the pavement to do something in the arts, and reluctantly took jobs as waiters and bartenders because they couldn't make anything happen? And you don't even know if you have to because you never even tried to pursue the one thing you actually care about. What is that?"

Shocked, she jumped up and shouted, "You're not my fucking family."

"Yes, yes I am. I'm your family right now. Me, Jason, even Pen, we are your family in every way that matters. They might be willing to let you float by for now, but not forever. That's not anger, so don't warp it in your mind. It's love. But you can't handle love, right?"

"You're talking out of your ass. My life is just the way I want it to be."

"I doubt that. You have some bullshit idea about who you are so you created a persona to match it, but it's all crap."

"Just get the fuck out."

"I must be getting close to something real, is that it?"

"You don't know what you're talking about," she insisted.

"Let's take your big obsession with the eighties, for example."

"I like the movies. So what?"

"Look a little deeper. It was all about big hair, big shoulder pads, and McMansions. But all of those big things covered up big lies. AIDS, inequality, all of it. Sometimes I think you are like the eighties. The quarterback shoulder pads don't fool me. What's behind all the lip gloss?"

"You're seeing things that aren't there. I like to party so I keep things simple."

Aidan shook his head. "I'll never get through to you."

"Just go. We're done."

As she heard the words come out of her mouth she gasped a little. She looked at Aidan to see what he would do.

"You hurt me tonight. Do you get that?" he asked softly.

She didn't know what to say, so she said nothing.

"I would let it go if I wasn't convinced it will happen again. Until you confront your demons, I know I'm only ever going to get glimpses of the real Tash, the one that hides in the MoMA film room and befriends a homeless man. The other version of you, what you show everyone else, she's just a shadow. I'm not willing to chase a shadow anymore."

Tash looked down.

Aidan pulled a copy of *Looking for Alaska* off of her dresser. "I know you've read this half a dozen times," he said, waving it around. "But you missed the point. Smoking to die isn't cool. It didn't make the character fun and mysterious. It's sad. Not romantic sad, just pathetic sad."

Tash looked perplexed.

Aidan put the book down and walked over to her, kneeling on the floor in front of her. "Listen to me. I love you as you really are, but you can't sit on the sidelines anymore."

She shook her head and turned away.

"You live at the edge of living, terrified to go after anything you actually want. Or even to figure out what you want. Why don't you think you're worth taking a chance on? If I do, why don't you?"

She looked him directly in the eyes, and said, "Stop your psychobabble and get out my apartment. We're over."

He stood up and looked at her, giving her a chance to take back her words.

"I never loved you. Get out."

He turned and left the room, gently shutting the bedroom door behind him.

A few minutes later, Jason knocked on her bedroom door.

"I'm so sorry; did we wake you up?"

"Don't worry about it. What happened?"

"It's over. I told Coconut Boy to leave."

"Sweetie, I know you're upset, but don't call him that. His name is Aidan."

CHAPTER 7

Penelope opened her eyes at the crack of dawn. *This comforter is like a cloud*, she thought, knowing it would be the last time she'd wake up there. She quietly shimmied out of bed and got dressed. As she grabbed her backpack and started walking to the door, a voice called behind her, "You're sneaking out?"

Pausing at the door, she turned around and said, "I meant what I said. I can't do this anymore. It's not who I am. Please don't contact me again."

"But…"

"But nothing. You're married and you know it's much worse than that."

"You know my marriage isn't real. As for the rest of it…"

"Please, I never should have let this continue once I learned everything. We both know it's well past time."

"Look, I know we weren't meant to last forever. But I'm concerned about what I have brought to your life. If I had known. I feel like I put you in an impossible situation and that wasn't my intention."

"You didn't."

"Penelope, please don't regret anything. You're very special and I'm grateful that you reminded me of what I was missing. I care deeply about you."

Penelope tilted her face shyly downward. "I'm grateful to you too. You'll always be my first, well, my first everything. But I need to move on and do what makes sense. Goodbye, Richard."

*

As Penelope left the hotel, she noticed the gardeners watering the bright red flowers that flanked the entrance. She was overcome by memories of the flowers at her father's bed and breakfast. On her way home, she thought back to that first day and everything that had happened since. She hoped that by remembering it all she could achieve closure.

75

It all began with a dreaded trip nearly one year ago during her summer break. Penelope was visiting her father for a week in Stowe, Vermont. As she pulled into the driveway of the large, refurbished Victorian, she wondered how she would survive a full week. While it was a magical place for those seeking a romantic getaway, for Penelope's father, it was a hideaway.

Throughout college and graduate school, she never scheduled Friday classes. This allowed her to visit for at least one long weekend each month, but full weeks were harder to bear. As she sat in her parked car, dragging her feet on going inside, she thought about how fatigued she felt after those long weekends. Tash once suggested that she "stop going so much because it's too far away and lame."

Penelope had responded, "He needs me. Since my mom, you know?"

Tash never mentioned it again. As Penelope sat there, she wondered if things would be different had she confided in Tash about how hard things really were. Lost in her thoughts, she didn't notice her father until he tapped on the car window, startling her. After catching her breath, she smiled at him and popped her trunk.

"Hey, Dad," she said as she emerged from her car.

Already leaning into the trunk to collect her luggage, he mumbled, "Hi, Honey."

As they walked into the house, her father remarked, "You seemed deep in thought."

"Just a long drive."

"Well, come on in and have a snack. I just put the afternoon refreshments out in the library."

"Okay. I'll unpack and come down."

"Here," her father said, handing her a key. "I had to put you on the third floor this time. It's a full house all week."

Penelope nodded as she took the key. She followed her father up the dark mahogany staircase, smiling politely while passing an elderly couple on their way down. As she entered the small room that featured a rickety canopy bed and flowered wallpaper, she felt envious of her friends who were returning home for the summer to their own bedrooms.

"I'll just put these here," her father said, placing her suitcase and backpack on a bench at the end of the bed. "This one is heavy," he continued, gesturing at the backpack.

"I have a lot of reading to do for school."

"Aren't classes over for the semester?"

"It's for my thesis. I'm supposed to present a proposal to the committee in the fall."

"Ah. Well, get settled in and I'll see you in a bit."

As he closed the door, she had two thoughts. *He forgot to hug me. This room is stuffy.*

*

Half an hour later, Penelope sat in the library sipping a glass of lemonade. Guests roamed about, occasionally stopping in to pick up a cool drink or a maple scone that paled in comparison to her mother's. Soon her father found her.

"Let's sit down and catch up," he said.

"Sure. Do you want to go sit outside on the porch swing?"

"Okay."

Penelope followed her father outside, glass of lemonade in hand.

As they sat on the swing it swayed, as if mimicking the unease they felt, but it soon steadied with their weight.

"So, the business is going well?" Penelope asked.

"We've been booked solid every weekend since the season began, and we're quite busy during the weeks as well. There was a lull between the end of the ski season and the start of summer, but that's normal."

"Uh huh," Penelope said, in an attempt to show she was paying attention.

"I've been toying with the idea of doing some kitchen renovations. We'll see. How's that lemonade? I squeezed it myself."

"Oh, it's good," Penelope said, taking a sip of the overly tart beverage.

"So, how are things in New York?"

"Pretty good."

"The apartment?"

"It's great. I spend a lot of time hanging out with my roommates. You remember that Tash is a big movie buff so we have a lot of movie nights. Kind of reminds me of when I was little."

"I still wish you would've gotten the other apartment, in the building with the doorman. New York isn't safe and you shouldn't get complacent."

"It's fine, Dad, really. You shouldn't worry."

"What about school?"

"Everything's good. I just have to finalize my thesis topic and get it approved. I've narrowed it down to representations of the Greek goddesses in contemporary art, but it's still too broad. Tash thinks I should focus on Persephone because she's kind of a rebel, but I'm leaning more towards Demeter, her mother, the goddess of the earth and harvest. Do you know the story about how she made the land desolate and barren each winter out of grief? She…"

"Honey, I have to run inside and check on the laundry machine. A guest needed it earlier, and, well, it doesn't matter. You stay here and enjoy the fresh air. I'll see you at dinner."

As he jumped up, the swing again swayed, this time taking longer to steady.

Penelope went to her room, where she napped and read before joining her father for a late dinner after he was done attending to his guests for the day. The dining room was only used to serve breakfast, and Ted avoided sullying the table linens by eating in the outdated kitchen instead, even when Penelope visited. He was able to fake his way through a couple of breakfast classics for his guests, but he was such a poor cook that after a year of eating frozen dinners he hired a local woman to deliver homemade, family-style meals once a week. This week it was roast beef, something neither he nor Penelope particularly enjoyed.

"Her roast turkey is top notch. The sides too. I should have asked her to make that for your visit," Ted said, noticing Penelope moving the food around on her plate.

"It's fine, Dad. I'm just not very hungry."

Although he was making an effort, Penelope was preoccupied with her greatest fear: she would have to accept her father as he now was, a man she hardly knew in a place she hardly belonged.

The next four days passed, each undifferentiated from the ones before. Penelope woke up at five o'clock to help her father prepare breakfast for the guests, which they served from six to nine, followed by an hour of cleaning. Then she read, drank afternoon lemonade, napped, read some more, and ate roast beef with her father, which, like their strained conversation, became increasingly difficult to digest. On the fifth day, everything changed.

*

The howling winds the night before forced her to shut her window, so Penelope was scarcely able to sleep at all in her stuffy room. She dragged herself down to the kitchen at five o'clock to find her father desperately searching in the cabinet under the sink.

"Morning, Dad. What are you looking for?" she asked sleepily.

"Flashlights. I can't find enough for all the guests."

"What? Why do we need flashlights?"

"The forecast changed overnight and the storm they thought was going to miss us is heading this way in full force. Hurricane winds, torrential downpours, and lightning are expected to start mid-afternoon," he said as he moved on to the pantry.

Penelope poured herself a cup of coffee, unbothered. "We probably won't lose power, Dad."

"I just want to be prepared. Check the freezer for batteries."

"The freezer?"

"They last longer there."

After locating the needed flashlights and batteries, Penelope and her father proceeded to make, serve, and clear breakfast. Penelope created emergency kits with flashlights and bottled water for each hotel guest, just in case. Concerned that the quickly dropping temperatures would make the place unseasonably chilly, Ted built a fire in the library fireplace. Penelope set out a platter of marshmallows and skewers to make the storm fun for the guests. From that point on, Penelope's day was no different from the days before, except the comfort she felt listening to the teeming rain outside. The conversation with her father was limited to weather reports he was reading on his smart phone.

Claiming he was exhausted from the long day, Ted retired immediately after dinner. Penelope washed the dishes and then searched the freezer for something sweet. She found a carton of Neapolitan ice cream tucked away in the back and opened it to discover the chocolate was gone. *It figures*, she thought. There was a frost-covered block of strawberry and vanilla left. After scraping away the freezer burn on the top, she put the rest in a bowl, grabbed her book, and went to curl up in the armchair by the fireplace. She was taking her last bite of ice cream when the bells on the front door rang out. She walked to the opening of the room and saw a well-dressed, middle-aged man standing in the entryway, dripping from head to toe.

"Can I help you?" she asked.

"I hope so. I have a vacation house about two miles away and we lost power. My back-up generator died after an hour. I usually only come up here during ski season and I guess I neglected to have the tank filled. I need a room for the night," he said, as she noticed the puddle he was creating as he stood there.

"Uh, my dad said all the rooms are filled but I can go wake him up and ask," she said.

"I wouldn't want you to do that. I'll find someplace else."

As he started to leave, sloshing with each step, Penelope said, "It's too dangerous to drive. Please come in and I'll get you some towels to dry off and a cup of tea or something. You can sit by the fire. I can fix the couch for you if that would be okay for the night."

"I wouldn't want to put you out."

"No, it's fine. Just stay put and I'll be back in a jiffy."

Penelope returned a few minutes later with a stack of towels and some bedding. "Here, take off your coat and dry off with these."

As she fitted the couch with sheets she said, "You'll be toasty in here by the fire. Can I get you some tea or coffee?"

"Tea would be lovely if it isn't too much trouble."

"No trouble. Are you hungry? We have some leftover roast beef, which I have to confess isn't very good. There are also some scones and muffins."

"Just the tea. Thank you."

Penelope returned ten minutes later holding a silver tray with a full tea service and a small plate of chocolate chip cookies.

"I found these in the cookie jar, in case you changed your mind and wanted a snack."

"Thank you. Do people really have cookie jars?" he asked.

"I guess people in Vermont do."

"I sense you're not from here?"

"No. I'm originally from Boston but I go to graduate school in New York City, at NYU. I come up here to visit my father from time to time."

"I live in the city as well. Normally, I only come up here with my son during the winter to ski."

"What brings you up here now?" she asked as she poured him a cup of tea.

"Truthfully, the short version is that I'm unhappy at home and wanted a change of scenery."

Pleasantly surprised by his candor, she asked, "What would the long version be?"

"An earful."

"I have time," Penelope said. "Uh, that is if you want to talk. I'm sorry, I'm being horribly rude. I've forgotten my manners altogether," she said, jumping up.

"Not at all."

"I should let you warm up and get some rest."

"Please, stay. Here, join me for a cup of tea," he said, lifting the teapot.

Penelope smiled and sat down.

"Do you take sugar or milk?" he asked.

She shook her head.

"What's your name?" he asked as he handed her the teacup.

"Penelope. And yours?"

"Richard."

Penelope took a sip of tea and said, "I don't want to pry, but you said…"

"That I'm unhappy at home."

She nodded. "I'm a good listener, that's all."

"Well," he said with a sigh, "where to begin?"

Over the next hour, Richard told Penelope that his twenty-year marriage was a sham. He revealed that he went out on a few dates with his wife because he was "never a ladies man and lacked the experience to know that indifference was a red flag." When she became pregnant and insistent on having the child, he felt marrying her was the right thing to do.

He explained, "I look back and see that I had other choices, but shall we say, appearances are very important in my family. At the time, it seemed easier to marry her and try to create a life together. Foolish."

Penelope listened sympathetically, thinking how lonely he must be, and how in her own way she could relate. She realized that she hadn't felt this connected to anyone in a long time.

She asked, "Have you ever thought about ending the marriage?"

He nodded. "I could never bring myself to do it though. I used to justify staying because I focused on my son and trying to keep his home together. The truth is that I feel sorry for my wife. We don't have any relationship to speak of, not even a friendship, but she's had a troubled life. The shell of the marriage is somehow important to her."

"And for you?"

He chuckled and shook his head. "I'm not used to people asking how I feel. Well, for me the shell is just what a shell is: empty."

"I'm sorry," Penelope said, unsure of herself.

"Please, don't feel sorry for me. My life has mainly been about my career and there's no one to blame for that but myself. The truth is that I'm probably not an emotionally giving person. Maybe the real reason I stayed all these years is because there is a part of me that is more comfortable with the façade. I don't know if I'd be any good at the real thing."

"Don't you want to find out though?" He smiled but before he could respond, she said, "Oh God, I'm sorry. That was inappropriate."

"No, don't be sorry. It's a thought I've had myself. That's really why I'm up here. I needed to escape to somewhere other than my office for a few days. You're remarkably easy to talk to. Believe it or not, I'm usually quite reserved."

She smiled. "Me too. I'm a good listener though."

"You also sound like quite a romantic. Is there someone special back in New York?"

"Oh, no, not at all. I mean no to both. I'm not seeing anyone and I'm not much of a romantic. I mean, I just never prioritized that stuff, but..."

"But?"

"My parents were very much in love, so maybe there's a part of me that at least believes that kind of movie love is possible. But it's not for me."

"Why not?"

She paused and set her teacup on the silver tray. "Would you like something stronger than tea? I think there's a bottle of brandy around here somewhere."

"Yes. Thank you."

Penelope returned a few minutes later with two brandy snifters.

"Cheers," they said as they clinked glasses.

"That's good," Richard said as he took a sip. "You know, the amber color is a bit like your eyes."

Penelope blushed.

"I'm sorry. I don't mean to make you uncomfortable."

"You didn't. I'm not used to people noticing things like that. Most people just see my glasses and don't even know what color my eyes are."

"You're very beautiful. I'd imagine there are guys your age lined up for you."

"Hardly," she said as she took a swig. "I'm sort of invisible to most guys, which suits me just fine."

"You were saying that before, that you're not a romantic."

"My mother died when I was in high school and it destroyed my father."

"I'm sorry. Was she ill?"

"No, it was a car accident – some reckless person, texting. My dad became a different person overnight. A shell of who he used to be. I guess I don't want to open myself up for that kind of hurt."

"Take it from me: avoiding love doesn't spare you from pain. At a minimum, it creates a slow but persistent numbing that might be worse than actual pain."

Penelope took another sip of her drink. "I've been focusing on my studies anyway."

"That's right; you said you're in graduate school. Why did you pick New York?"

"I wanted to change my life I guess. Take more chances. But I haven't really changed like I hoped."

"Change is hard. What are you studying?"

"Art history."

They talked for hours about art, literature, and mythology. Richard was well-versed in every subject that came up, which he chalked up to "a good education." They batted around some of Penelope's thesis ideas and Richard suggested she read the work of Sarah Cohen, a feminist historian who has written about the goddesses in modernity. When Penelope asked how he was familiar with her work, he hesitated a bit before saying, "My wife has taken me to some book events."

"Oh," she said, unable to conceal her irrational disappointment. After a moment passed, Penelope said, "It must be really late."

Richard looked at his watch. "God, it's after two. I shouldn't have kept you so long."

Penelope stood up. "I should let you get some rest. I have to be up in a few hours to help my dad with breakfast. Please join us whenever you wake up."

Richard stood up and put his hand out.

Penelope extended her arm in anticipation of a handshake, but instead he took her hand and clasped it in his. They stood for a moment, the only noise the last crackles from the dying embers of the fire.

"Well, goodnight," she said.

"Goodnight." It seemed as though he wanted to say more, but he didn't.

Penelope went to her room where she lay wide-eyed, wondering what had just happened and trying to understand what she was feeling. *He's so average looking and he's old; why am I thinking about him? He's obviously having a midlife crisis. But he has kind eyes, and he seemed to get me – really get me – and I think I got him. What was that?*

After a sleepless night, she rolled out of bed at five o'clock and headed down to the kitchen. *Dad must have slept in. Wonder what he'll say about Richard sleeping on our couch*, she thought as she started the coffee pot. She noticed that the two brandy glasses had been cleaned and placed in the drying rack, so she walked into the library to check on Richard. He was gone. The bedding was folded neatly, and atop it, she found a note.

Thank you for your hospitality and for listening. Forgive me for overstepping, but my failures have opened my eyes and so I want to offer you some advice. Open your heart to somebody, someday. They will be very lucky. You deserve all life has to offer. Richard.

She smiled as she held the paper, the faint smell of last night's fire still in the air.

"Penelope, there you are," her father said from the doorway. "I saw you started the coffee. You look tired. Did you get any sleep or did the wind keep you up too?"

"Uh, no. I didn't get much sleep."

*

Two months later, Penelope was crouching on the floor of the Fifth Avenue Barnes & Noble looking at Moleskine notebooks when she heard, "Penelope?"

She looked up to see Richard. She smiled as he reached his hand out to pull her up, her skin sparking when it touched his.

"Hi, Richard."

"Buying a notebook?" he asked.

"Oh, yeah. It's a start-of-the-semester ritual. I pick a different color each time."

"It's reassuring to know people still buy non-electronic notebooks."

"What about you?" she asked, sheepishly.

"I just left a meeting nearby and stopped in to get a birthday card for my sister."

Penelope smiled softly. "I wondered if I'd ever see you again. Every time I visit my father and someone walks through the front door, I look to see if it's you, which I know is stupid because you have a house down the road and…"

"It's not stupid. I've wondered if I would see you again, too."

"You left in the middle of the night. Was your power restored?"

"Actually, I drove back to the city."

"In that awful storm?"

"I wanted to do it before I lost my nerve."

"To do what?" she asked.

"Change my life."

She paused before asking, "And did you?"

He looked down and shook his head. "My wife lost her job. If you asked her, she would say that she made a career change, but that's par for the course. Her career was all she had. We're two of a kind that way. It wasn't the right time."

"I'm sorry."

"Don't be. You helped me more than you know."

Penelope smiled. After an awkward moment, she said, "Well, I guess I should buy my notebook."

"Are you in a hurry? Maybe you'd like to get a drink or a bite to eat. I owe you for the tea and brandy."

"Oh, well, uh…" she stuttered.

"It's all right if you'd rather not. I hope this doesn't sound strange but I felt a connection with you that I haven't felt before, so seeing you again is remarkable."

"I felt the same way."

"Shall we then?"

"Yes. Let's," she said without hesitation.

Penelope helped Richard find a suitable birthday card, after which he insisted on buying her new midnight blue notebook. As they stepped onto a bustling Fifth Avenue, Penelope asked, "Where should we go?"

"We're a few blocks from The Plaza. The Rose Club has a great wine list. Have you been there?"

She shook her head. "Would it be pathetic to say that I was obsessed with the *Eloise* books as a child? I've always hoped for an excuse to go there."

He smiled. "The Plaza it is."

She spent the next week consumed by anticipation and worry. *What have I gotten myself into?* When Friday came, Penelope laid potential outfits all over her bed. She tried on jeans with several different t-shirt and blazer combinations, overcome by disappointment each time she looked in the mirror. *If I want to be less serious and have more fun, I need to change it up. I just need to get outside of myself.* After spending an hour trying on everything in her closet, she settled on a simple white sundress, far more frivolous than her daily attire. On her way out the door, she panicked and grabbed a blue cardigan, rationalizing that she didn't want to be cold.

She arrived at The Paris and was relieved to see Richard waiting for her, tickets in hand.

"You look lovely," he said as he handed her a ticket.

"Oh, thank you," she said, hoping he wouldn't notice her sweaty palms.

They stepped into the crowded line of moviegoers, slowly making their way into the sold-out theater. Penelope's heart raced; she wasn't sure if it was the crowds, Richard, or both. As the smell of buttered popcorn wafted into her nostrils, she stole a glance at Richard. *With just one change, the familiar can be made unfamiliar.*

"What about over there?" he asked, pointing to two seats in the dead center of the theater.

"Perfect." Other patrons stood up to let them wriggle into the row, so he took her hand and led her to their seats. After some small talk about their days, the lights went out. They sat in the glow of the screen, and Penelope made a conscious decision to let go and lose herself in the movie, something she wasn't accustomed to. By the end, she had a palpable lump in her throat. Unable to speak, she turned to face Richard and smiled, teary eyed. He gently rubbed her hand.

After they made their way outside Richard said, "The Plaza is right here. Should we go for that hot chocolate?"

Penelope nodded. *Could he be what I was waiting for? Maybe this is my chance to change my life.*

They entered the grand lobby for the second time, and Richard took her hand.

He pointed and said, "I think the hot chocolate is over there."

"What if we get room service instead?" Penelope's words surprised even her. *Who am I? I can't believe I said that.*

He nodded. "Stay here for a minute."

He returned a few moments later with a room key. They held hands during the impossibly long elevator ride, each watching the changing numbers as if afraid to look at each other.

They entered the room in silence and stood next to the bed, still holding hands. Richard stroked Penelope's cheek, leaned in, and kissed her. He took her sweater off and the strap from her sundress slipped off her shoulder. He touched her shoulder and she felt a shiver. They made love that night.

When she awoke the next morning, she suddenly wondered, *Was that a one-night stand? My first time can't be a one-night stand in a hotel. I think I feel different. Everything feels kind of different. Or do I just want it to?*

Richard looked over and said, "Good morning. Did you sleep well?"

"Uh huh."

Richard caressed her face and she averted her eyes.

"What is it? What's wrong?"

"You're married. I'm just wondering if you do this kind of thing often."

He shook his head. "I promise, not once in all of these years. And I didn't mean for this to happen with us, but I'm glad it did. Are you?"

She nodded.

"How about I order some breakfast and we can decide what landmark we're going to visit next?"

She was surprised that he'd thought of their plan.

"Remember? We said we'd see the sites from our favorite books and films."

"I remember," she said.

Over the next several months, they visited the Empire State Building, Central Park, and Times Square. Penelope particularly enjoyed going to museums together so she could teach Richard about the origins of the paintings and their historical significance. They saw *The Woman in Gold* at the Neue Galerie and Van Gogh's *The Starry Night* at the MoMA. While standing before Van Gogh's masterpiece, she realized it was the closest she had come to looking at the stars in years and she felt grateful. After their outings, they always returned to The Plaza, which had become "their place." Since Richard didn't appear to have any worries about going out with her in public, she chose to forget that he was married.

She spent increasingly less time with her roommates, who were busy with their own lives and didn't seem to notice. Her schoolwork suffered a little and her thesis proposal was past due, but as a lifelong overachiever, she felt entitled to a break.

Everything changed on Valentine's Day. Penelope was approaching her apartment after class, trying not to slip on the veneer of frost covering the sidewalk. To her surprise, she saw Richard standing outside of her building. He looked startled to see her.

"Penelope! What are you doing here?"

"You're not here to see me?" she asked, bewildered.

"No. Is this where you live?"

She nodded. "What are you doing here?"

"I'm taking my son Kyle out to dinner, but he wanted to stop by his cousin's place to drop off a gift. She recently broke up with someone and he wanted to make sure someone gave her a Valentine's gift."

Oh my God. It can't be, she thought, trembling.

"That name never meant anything to me before, but..." she mumbled incoherently.

"What are you talking about, Penelope? Do you know Kyle?"

"What's your niece's name?" she asked with dread.

"Natashya."

"Oh my God."

"You know her?"

"Tash is my roommate and she's going to kill me."

*

Over the next few months, Penelope started to unravel. For the first time in her life, even when she hunkered down at the library, she was unable to concentrate. She was racked with guilt, exacerbated every time she saw Tash, who was more protective of Kyle than anyone. Terrified she would confess the affair and ruin everyone's lives, Penelope avoided Tash, which meant avoiding Jason as well. Their movie nights and roommate talks became a thing of the past. Worse, Tash and Jason didn't seem to miss her. Penelope felt utterly alone. Richard was the only person she could talk to, which made ending it with him seem impossible. Now afraid to be caught together in public, they saw each other less frequently and only at The Plaza.

It all came to a head as the spring slipped into summer. Richard insisted that it was time to tell his wife. "We can't go on like this. You're too afraid to go anywhere and this feels wrong."

"Please don't. If you do, Kyle will surely find out and then it's only a matter of time before Tash finds out. We haven't been terribly close recently, but she's probably still my best friend. If she hates me, Jason will too. I will lose everything."

"Kyle won't find out. My wife would never tell him and neither would I."

"You don't know that. Besides, I don't want to be the cause of a marriage ending, whether it's a good marriage or not."

"You're not the cause. I've wanted to do this for a long time, since before we met."

"We should split up, just end things. Then you can do what you want and it will have nothing to do with me."

Richard shook his head. He looked broken.

"I'm ashamed I didn't end this sooner," she said, unable to make eye contact.

"Listen to me. I won't do anything, and you don't either. Let's just take some time and sort things out. See where the chips fall. Please."

Emotionally drained, Penelope agreed. In the coming weeks, she tried to pull herself together and look at things rationally. She hoped to make progress on her thesis but was entirely too preoccupied. Then one day Richard texted to say that he wanted to see her. She knew when she left the library to meet him that she would end the relationship once and for all.

As the cab pulled up to her apartment building in the early morning light after her last night with Richard, she had one thought: *Should I tell Tash?*

CHAPTER 8

Oh shit, Jason thought as he approached the Battery Park set and saw Sam at the makeup tent. *I wonder if he still thinks I'm a jerk. Tash would have a field day with this. I hope she's okay.*

"Hey," Sam said as he pulled out a folding chair for Jason.

"Hey, dude. Uh, I mean Sam. Hey, Sam."

Sam smiled as Jason silently berated himself. *What's wrong with me? He's just the makeup guy. Don't let him rattle you.*

"They want to get started as soon as possible in case we go long. So Tanya here is going to do your hair while I do your face. Your makeup! While I do your makeup," Sam said, looking flushed.

"Cool. Hi, Tanya," Jason said with a nod. *Hmm, Sam seems nervous. He remembers. I can almost hear Tash saying that he's probably worried you're going to get him fired.*

Soon they were doing the first set-up. Distracted with thoughts of Tash, Jason had trouble finding his light. He required repeated direction from the photographer. Sam noticed and requested they stop the shoot for a moment, pretending he needed to fix a stray eyelash on Jason's face.

When he got close to Jason, he whispered, "You seem a little off. Are you okay?"

"My best friend is in crisis, broke up with her guy last night. I'm preoccupied, I guess."

"Remember, you're the star. Tune it all out."

"Thanks, Sam."

Jason regrouped and was soon in the zone. He was egged on as the crowd of bystanders grew, necessitating the crew to put up more barricades. At the command of the photographer, Sam ran on set to do touch-up work.

"You're on fire now!" he said to Jason.

"Thanks, and for earlier too."

Sam smiled. "People are standing around, waiting for your autograph."

"Really, dude? I figured people stopped to see if anything looks exciting and they don't even know what it is."

"I heard some of them say your name. They know you," Sam said excitedly.

Jason smiled, but then caught himself, afraid to appear arrogant.

"You're all set. I'm jumping out."

"Cool. Thanks, Sam."

After another hour of shooting, they broke for lunch.

Jason bypassed the catered food and headed straight to his makeup chair. The rest of the crew ate their lunch together. Noticing Jason alone, Sam put his half-eaten tuna sandwich down, grabbed two bottles of water, and headed over to Jason.

"Thanks," Jason said as he took the water Sam offered.

"I'm sorry about your friend. I hope she's okay."

"She's going through some stuff and kind of fucking up her life, but she needs to figure it out for herself."

"Hopefully she will. Maybe you can nudge her in the right direction."

"You know what's funny is that we watch movies together all the time. She's one of my roommates. We watched *Desperately Seeking Susan* like a week ago. You know the old Madonna flick, back when people thought she'd always be ahead of the trends?"

Sam nodded.

"The big scenes all take place here in Battery Park, and now I'm here."

"Yeah, that's right. I watched it online a few years ago. What I remember most was Roberta, the desperate housewife, you know before there were desperate housewives. God, she was so lonely in her sad, orgasm-free suburban marriage."

Jason laughed. "At first it seemed like it's all about Madonna's fabulous lace bustiers and sequined boots, but then I wondered if each of us really has a person we would chase around the world, you know, like the Susan character. That one person you can't quite forget… Jeez, listen to me. Sorry. I guess I'm still thinking about my roommate."

Sam smiled. "So, are you one of those models who doesn't eat? They're going to call you back soon."

"Just not during shoots. Nerves."

Sam smirked.

"What?" Jason prodded.

"It always surprises me when guys like you get nervous."

"Guys like me?"

"Guys who've had it easy."

"Wow, that's a big assumption."

"I keep putting my foot in my mouth," Sam mumbled before backtracking. "I just meant that you seem like you have every reason to be confident."

"It's not like I've had any training for this. I never planned on becoming a model. Some guy approached me at a yoga studio. Turned out he worked for one of the biggest agents in the business. I didn't really know what I was in for."

"Is that regret? Seems like you have a pretty huge opportunity."

"No regret. I'm just saying I get nervous. Pretty sure one of these days, these people are gonna figure out that I don't belong here."

"I doubt it. You're a rising star."

"I'm a token, an experiment."

Sam looked perplexed.

"The only thing they like about me is my skin color. I'm just a trend that hasn't gone out of style yet, you know?"

"God, I feel like a jerk."

Jason laughed. "I'm not saying you should feel sorry for me. I have a sweet gig and I'm enjoying it. But it is what it is, you know?"

Sam nodded. "I bet people underestimate you."

At that moment, the photographer's assistant came to the tent to fetch Jason. As Jason walked back to the set, Sam called after him.

"What you asked before, about each person having someone they can't quite shake – I think we do, if we're lucky."

Jason smiled.

*

The shoot moved to the South Street Seaport and eventually the Circle Line Ferry, continuing until dusk, when the photographer finally lamented that there was no more usable light. Jason was ready to leave when he noticed Sam packing up.

"Sam, thanks again for everything today."

"My pleasure. You smashed it. And I hope your friend is okay."

"Would you, uh, that is if you don't have plans, would you like to go grab a bite to eat?"

"Are you asking me out?"

"Yeah," Jason replied.

"Well, I usually don't date models. You know, models always hang all over the makeup guys," he said, before bursting out into laughter.

Jason sighed.

"I was just kidding. I'm sorry. My timing is seriously off. Yes, I would love to go out with you, if you still want to."

Jason nodded.

"You must be starving. What are you in the mood for?"

"Ever since we talked about that movie, I've been craving Chinese food. Remember the scene where they get wasted and eat takeout on the roof?"

Sam smiled. "Chinatown it is."

*

"Do they really say that?" Sam asked as he took his last sip of hot and sour soup.

"Oh yeah. Sometimes I even hear the crew gossiping about me and they always say 'That one, the Chinese one.' And I'm like, my mom is Japanese and my dad is Korean. On what planet does that make me Chinese?"

"That's awful. Maybe it's the price to pay for breaking the stereotype."

"Most of the time I feel like a huge sellout. I've never said that to anyone before. I know it's a bullshit job and I let them use me, but it's such an easy way to make serious bank. To be honest, I don't know what I would have done if this hadn't landed in my lap. Most of my friends are struggling to make ends meet. Some had to move back home, couldn't survive in the city."

"I hear that. I lay awake some nights wondering how I'm going to pay my bills. My apartment is three hundred square feet and I can't afford it. The interest on my debt from my cosmetology program keeps growing and it seems like I'll never get ahead of it. I keep waiting for it to get just a little easier, but it never does."

"Why do you stay in the city?"

"It's oxygen. Survival. I'd do anything to stay here. You have to understand, I'm from a small town in Missouri where you lived in fear if people even suspected you were gay. I walked down the street with people following behind me, saying that they hoped I died of AIDS."

Jason listened intently, not taking his eyes off of Sam.

Sam continued, "I dreamed of making my way here someday. Cliché, I know, but for me New York represented more than a safe place; it was an idea, a concept. You know, the way America is an idea as much as a place. New York represents possibility. That idea got me through a hell that others didn't survive. As soon as I could afford a ticket, I left all that shit behind. Beating after beating, threat after threat, I found a way to survive. But I think if I gave up on the idea of New York now, well, I wouldn't survive that."

Jason outstretched his arm and put his hand on Sam's. At that moment, the waiter delivered the bill.

"Let me get this," Jason said as he snatched it up.

"I didn't mean…"

"I invited you out," Jason said.

As they left the restaurant Sam asked, "So now what?"

"Now how about you take me home to your tiny apartment?"

*

The next morning Jason woke up to the smell of French vanilla.

"I made coffee," Sam said from the galley kitchen. "Are you hungry or are you in a hurry?"

Jason thought for a moment. "Not in a hurry at all. Now come here and give me a kiss."

Sam prepared omelets while Jason showered. Over brunch they talked about photographers they like, the benefits of work travel, and books, discovering they both have an interest in architecture and design. Before Jason left, he invited Sam to a club opening the following night. Although he seemed surprised by the invitation, Sam agreed to meet him there.

When Jason got home late that afternoon, he bumped into Penelope.

"Hey, Pen."

When she turned, he could see she had been crying.

"Are you okay?" he asked.

"I'm fine," she sighed before closing the bathroom door.

Jason redirected his focus on Tash and knocked on her door.

"Come in."

He opened the door and walked right over to the bed, sitting on the corner.

"Hey sweetie," he said.

"Hey."

"You might want to get out of bed and start the day."

"I called out of work. I'm tired."

"Do you want to talk about what happened with Aidan?"

"No."

"There's something wrong with Pen. She looks like she's been crying all night. Do you know what's going on?"

Tash shook her head.

"Weeeeelll, then we can talk about me. Do you want to hear about the shoot?"

Tash sat up, leaning against the wall. "Wasn't that yesterday? Are you just getting back?"

"Uh huh. Remember that guy I met? Sam?"

Tash thought for a minute. "Makeup Boy?"

"We went out last night after the shoot and I stayed at his place."

"And you're just getting back now? Did you take downers and sleep all day?"

"No, he made me brunch."

"You stayed for brunch? Wow, so does this mean ugly sex is as hot as they say? You know, because they like try harder or something?"

"He's not ugly. He has great eyes, among other things."

"Oh my God," she said, perking up. "You actually like him!"

Jason smiled brightly.

"That's great, honey. But just remember, we're all tomorrow's discards. I wouldn't get too heavy."

"Sweetie, you have to call Aidan."

PART THREE

CHAPTER 9

"Since you're actually on time this morning you can help me open the shop."

Fine, oh passive aggressive one, Tash thought. "What do you want me to do?" she asked from the customer couch she was slumped in.

"Clean the jewelry case. A customer's child got finger-prints all over it yesterday."

She rolled her eyes and sluggishly made her way to the backroom to get the cleaning supplies. Moving a Windex-soaked paper towel in circles over the glass case, she was completely detached from herself. Lost in rote movements and absent of discernible thoughts, she didn't realize that she was wiping the same spot on the counter over and over again. When Catherine called, "Tash, I'm opening," she was jarred back into the moment. *Great, another thrilling day begins.*

Inundated with the morning rush, Tash immediately started assisting customers. She was good at sizing people up and when she was attentive, customers were captivated by her. To them, Tash was the living embodiment of the confident, effortless style they were hoping to buy. When a young woman in a miniskirt came in, Tash pointed out each skirt in the store, explaining how flattering the cut is. Once in the dressing room with a pile of skirts, Tash assembled mix-and-match outfits and suggested additional pieces. "You look hot in that," she said, her standard phrase of encouragement. Her skills and charisma landed her the considerable sale.

Catherine said, "You know, you're very skilled with customers when you make an effort. If you made a bigger commitment to the store, you could be assistant manager someday."

"Thanks," she said, halfheartedly. *Then I can be just like you. Holy shit. I didn't think I could feel worse today.*

Deflated from the prospect of turning into Catherine, she returned to assisting customers. She rang up sales, issued store credits, answered calls, and ran back and forth from the register to the dressing rooms to the storeroom and back again. It was an utterly normal day.

When Catherine left to pick up lunch, Tash wandered aimlessly around, looking for an outfit to rehang or a display in need of adjustment. She thought about rearranging the new arrivals up front but didn't want to spur a lecture from Catherine. So she meandered back to the counter, her usual place for slouching and counting the minutes. Normally engrossed in making plans for her evenings, time moved far slower now that she was spending her nights alone at home. *It can't only be 12:05,* she thought as she glanced at the clock. *The days are getting longer. I wish there was at least a window display to create.*

Just when she thought she couldn't be any more bored, customers walked in. Like a switch going off in her mind, the ring of the door chime propelled Tash into a fantasy. In her mind's eye, the store suddenly turned into the scene of a musical. Everything was transformed into Technicolor and she envisioned herself screaming and then breaking out into dance and song. Customers became backup singers and mannequins swayed from side to side.

"Miss, do you have these pants in a smaller size?" a customer asked, instantly closing the curtain on her fantasy musical.

"Yes, ma'am. I'll go check in the back," she said.

Fuck, what's wrong with me? It's like I'm in a Björk video. God, who directed that video? It was so different than... fuck, snap out of it, she thought as she hit the side of her head.

She returned with the pants to find even more customers milling about. Soon Catherine returned and took charge, assisting the wealthiest-looking customers while Tash fetched different sizes from the back, cleaned out dressing rooms, and offered bottles of water to bored men waiting for their wives. The hours passed slowly.

She breathed a sigh of relief when it was finally time to clock out. On the walk home, she barely acknowledged the street vendors trying to catch her attention, too lethargic to offer a smile or even a sarcastic word. As she crossed over from SoHo into the Village, the city transitioned from work to play, with the sounds of friends meeting filling the air. The only thing Tash could concentrate on was crawling into bed and watching TV, her new nightly ritual that had taken the place of the club scene. As she approached Washington Square Park, she noticed Harold wrapping something around his ankle.

"Oh, hello Natashya."

"What's wrong with your ankle?" she asked, staring at the purple, swollen appendage.

"Had a little tussle," he said with a wince as he tried to wrap it with an old navy-blue bandana.

"Did someone do this to you?" she asked in outrage.

He shook his head. "A lovely young lady like you shouldn't worry. I'm fine."

"You need ice on that. Hang on and I'll run to the store."

"You needn't..." he tried to call after her but she was already on her way.

When she returned, she sat on the bench next to him and opened a plastic bag to reveal ice, baby wipes, and an Ace bandage. She opened the container of wipes and held it out.

"I thought it would be smart to clean it first," she said.

"Thank you," he said as he used one to wipe the dirt from his swollen ankle. "You didn't have to go to all this trouble. I can get by."

"I know," she said. "Do you remember the day we first met? I had twisted my ankle."

He nodded.

She opened a soda cup filled with ice. "It was the only way I could get some," she said. "Don't worry; I got some napkins we can put the ice in."

He offered a close-mouthed smile.

As he held the makeshift ice pack against his injured ankle, Tash quietly said, "Harold, I don't want to pry, but…"

"The time has come?"

She looked at him, uncertain of herself.

"Yes, you can ask me. Go ahead."

"How did you end up here?"

"I wish I could tell you the story you want to hear: a fairytale about the perfect life that unraveled because of one tricky bend in the path I didn't see coming. The career that toppled, the love of my life I lost, the children I miss. I long for that beautiful lie. But Miss Natashya, I have no such story."

"I'm sorry. I didn't mean to…"

He put his hand up. "I do not wish to be a cautionary tale for anyone. But if my story were told, it wouldn't be one of someone who lost it all, rather, someone who never wanted anything to lose."

Tash looked down and tried to make sense of what he was saying.

"I am quite content, most of the time," he said, returning his attention to his ankle.

She stood up and smiled. "Don't wrap the bandage too tightly. It should fit comfortably. You might want to save the rest of the wipes, you know, for whatever. There's a sandwich and a bottle of water in the bag."

"Thank you, Natashya," he said as he continued tending to his injury.

She took a few steps and considered saying something more, but decided against it and headed home. She dropped her bag inside her front door and dragged herself to the kitchen. She took a tub of Campbell's chicken noodle soup from the cabinet and stuck it in the microwave. As it cooked, she grabbed a Diet Coke and opened a jar of maraschino cherries, popping a couple directly into her mouth. She bit into the cherries, releasing their sugary liquid, and thought about how much she'd always loved them. When the microwave beeped, she stuck her soda under one arm and retrieved her soup and a spoon.

Both of her roommates' doors were closed. Jason must be out with Sam again, and Pen's probably locked in her room. When she got to her room, the floor covered with dirty laundry, she made space to put her food down on her nightstand before changing into her sweats. She crawled into bed, searched the sheets for her remote control, flipped on the TV, and started eating.

Afraid of bumping into Aidan at a club and too depressed to go out with friends, this had become her new nightly ritual. Jason spent most nights out with Sam, and although he invited her to join them many times, she didn't want to be a third wheel. Without plugging into the city's energy at night, her days felt longer and increasingly monotonous.

When he was home, Jason sat on her bed while she got ready to go to work in the mornings. She lived vicariously through his stories.

"I took Sam to a film screening at the SoHo House last night."

"What film?" she asked, searching for a clean tank top.

"I don't know. Some docu-whatever about eating disorders. It was a charity thing and my agent put me on the list."

"Kind of sketchy to send models to promote eating disorder awareness or whatever."

"Yeah, I know. Aaaaanyway, Sam is great in those places. He can talk to anyone and a lot of A-listers know him from work."

"Uh huh."

"I know it's early…"

"In the morning? Yeah, it is!" she said with a snicker.

"No, early in the relationship, smart ass," he said, tossing a wet towel at her.

"Okay, jeez, I'm listening. Early in the relationship for what?" she asked, still searching for a top.

"To think it might be something. It's good for me to be with someone like him. Someone, um, down to earth."

"First of all, it's not early in the relationship by your slutty standards; it's shockingly far into it."

He laughed.

Second, he's so lucky to have you. Seriously."

Jason smiled.

"Shit, now I'm gonna be late for work again. Help me find a shirt."

*

"Tash is always in and out of relationships. They never last, but she's sort of a love junkie…"

"Or maybe a love seeker," Sam suggested.

"Yes! You nailed it," Jason agreed and took his hand as they walked into Minetta Tavern. Recognizing Jason, the hostess immediately showed them to a reserved section of the bar. "We have a nice semi-round in the dining room ready when your friends arrive."

"Thank you," Jason replied as he and Sam hopped on barstools.

"This place is cool," Sam said, looking around. "You'd never expect this when you walk in."

"They have the best high-end cheeseburgers in the city," Jason said.

"You eat burgers?" Sam asked skeptically.

"Once in a blue moon."

"You never finished telling me about your roommate and her relationship drama."

"Actually, what I wanted to tell you was more about me, well, us I guess," he said, putting his hand on Sam's thigh.

"I'm listening."

"This is the first time I've done the healthy relationship thing. It's amazing. *You're* amazing, Sam. You're good for me."

Sam put his hand over Jason's hand and smiled softly.

"Listen, we're having a great time, but it isn't too heavy, right? I mean, we're keeping it light?"

"Uh, yeah. Of course. We're just having fun," Jason stammered, trying to cover his confusion.

"I mean, I'm not seeing anyone else. How could I? We're always together. But it's meant to be a good time. We're on the same page, right?"

"Definitely," Jason said.

Their friends arrived just in time to rescue Jason from the uncomfortable spotlight. Sam leapt off his stool to give them hugs while Jason sat thinking, *Not too heavy? Keep it light? What exactly does he mean?*

As the group settled in at their table, Jason excused himself to use the men's room. He splashed cold water on his face, wishing he could go back in time and wash the heart off his sleeve.

*

A few weeks later, Tash received a text from Kyle asking her to meet for lunch. She was reluctant because she didn't want to talk about Aidan, and Kyle could always tell when she was in a bad space. But it would be nice to see him, so she agreed to meet at their favorite diner the next day.

"Damn! I'm perfectly on time and was hoping to surprise you by beating you here for a change," Tash said as she hugged Kyle.

"You get credit for being on time," he said as they slid into the booth.

The waitress tried to hand them oversized laminated menus, but Kyle stopped her. "We actually know what we want: two coffees and a platter of blueberry blintzes to share, please."

As the waitress walked away, Tash said, "She's new, not like the other dinosaurs here. She looks like she's our age. God, that's depressing. Can you imagine working here?"

The waitress returned with their coffee and a plate of complimentary bagel chips. As they fixed their coffee, Tash asked, "What's been going on?"

"Summer kind of sucks. I'm living back at home, which is a major drag.

"That blows," Tash said as she searched for a cinnamon raisin bagel chip.

Now that my mom is a literary agent, she's working for herself so she's always home."

"That totally sucks."

"Yup."

"Does she like being an agent at least? Being your own boss sounds cool."

"She was pretty stoked that she landed a big deal for one of her clients. Some unknown guy, Pete Rice. His book is called *The Lost Notebooks* and she got him a deal with Random House. I guess it's her first big score. We got Chinese food to celebrate, which was lame."

Tash giggled.

"There's definitely something up with my parents though."

"You said that when I saw you last time."

"Being at home, I'm certain. It's obvious. I don't know what happened but they don't talk at all. I mean, not a word. It's creepy."

"No offense, but they've always been kinda messed up."

"Yeah, I know."

"So, you seeing anyone?" she asked.

Kyle shook his head.

The waitress interrupted to deliver their blintzes with two small plates for sharing. They each took a blintz and a dollop of sour cream. Kyle asked, "What's been going on with you?"

"These look really hot," Tash said as she cut into a blintz and watched the creamy filling ooze out.

Kyle put his fork down and looked intently at Tash. "Okay, what's wrong?"

"Why do you think…"

He shook his head. "Just tell me."

"Aidan and I broke up."

"When?"

"A few weeks ago," she replied before taking a bite of her blintz.

"What happened?"

"It's a long story," she said with a full mouth.

Kyle continued staring at her, tilting his head slightly as a means of gently prodding her.

She eventually threw her fork down. "Fine. It was stupid. I drank a little too much and danced with some guy at a club and it caused all of this drama."

"Some guy?"

"Some club promoter Aidan was kind of interviewing with."

"Oh, Tash."

"Whaaat? Don't 'Oh, Tash' me. He totally overreacted and said all of this awful stuff to me."

"Like what?"

"Crap about how I hide behind a persona like I'm fake or something. And how I'm wasting my life and don't go after my dreams."

"Well?"

"Well what?" she snapped.

"Hey, I love you but it sounds like he's just calling you on your shit, right?"

She didn't respond.

"And getting drunk and dancing with the club promoter? Really?"

"Why are you judging me and taking his side?"

"I'm always on your side. You know that. But what you did at the club isn't who you are, so what's really going on?"

"What are you talking about? You know better than anyone how I am when I'm out having fun."

"That's how you used to be; it's not who you are now. And for the record, I never thought that was how you were when you were truly having fun. I always thought that's how you acted to look like you were having fun."

"Sometimes it's hard to tell the difference," she said softly.

"Listen, I remember the assholes you dated in college, and I remember how they treated you. Aidan seemed really different, like he gets you."

"Wait," she said with a laugh. "You never like the guys I date."

"Exactly."

*

As she walked home in the summer heat, the foul smell of garbage permeating the air, she replayed Kyle's words. *It's not who you are. Then who the hell am I?* she wondered. The rumble of the subway caused the ground beneath her feet to vibrate and she was reminded of the sound of film spinning in the old projection rooms she visited during college. She started to imagine her life, frame by frame, whirling in front of her. Lost in thought as she walked down Macdougal Street, she paused when she noticed the rare music store an old boyfriend worked at was out of business. With Kyle's words still ringing in her ears, she saw a new series of images from a horrible New Year's Eve years earlier.

Drunk and high on pot and ecstasy, she and her boyfriend passed out in his bedroom after a party. She awoke the next morning, naked and lying between him and his lecherous roommate, with no memory of what happened, nor any doubt. It was unfolding again before her eyes in a series of visceral flashes. Pulling the dirty sheets up to her chin to cover her cold body. The stale smell of pot and cigarettes in the air. Pretending to sleep while he lay there. Chills going up her body but feeling too afraid to move to get her clothes. Trying not to even breathe. The lump forming in her throat, moving into her chest, like a vice getting tighter and tighter. Exhaling when he finally woke up and left the room.

As the flashes came faster and faster, she quickened her pace, as if trying to outwalk the images. But she couldn't outpace them. She remembered frantically searching in her pocketbook for cab fare to get home, only to realize that he had also stolen from her. *He took whatever he wanted.* The intense humiliation.

Wondering, *Why do I care about cab fare? What's wrong with me?* She shuddered as she remembered boasting to her friends about what a "killer party" it had been, too afraid to say the truth aloud. The physical hurt. The wretched soreness that worsened the next day. The unbearable fear that it would never get better. The worry of disease.

Deep in thoughts she was trying to escape, she approached Washington Square Park and didn't notice Harold until he spoke to her.

"Hello, Ms. Natashya," he said.

She stopped to chat, still breathing rapidly. "Oh, hi, Harold. How's your ankle?"

"Better. Haven't seen you in a few weeks," he said.

"Been busy. I'll bring you coffee soon."

"Lovely. And your young man? Haven't seen him around here lately."

"Oh screw you!"

CHAPTER 10

Every day for the next week, Tash looked for Harold on the way to and from work, hoping to apologize. Twice she brought donuts but there was no sign of him. *He's been gone a long time. Even when they run him off, he's usually not gone this long. I wonder if he's okay,* she thought. *I shouldn't have been such a bitch.*

She gave up on finding him for the moment and went home. She tossed her bag toward the common room love seat and watched it land on the floor. She left it, intending to head to her room, but wound up standing in Jason's doorway. He was lying on his bed and watching old cartoons.

"What are you watching?" she asked with an attitude.

"*Rainbow Bright*. She's amazing, and she's totally gay!"

Tash smirked. "I think rainbows used to be just rainbows."

"No way. I'm telling you, totally gay. Anyway, I needed something upbeat."

"Well, you picked the right thing. Why? What's up?"

"Relationship stuff. I don't know. I may be misreading something. Trying not to think about it and just chill."

"I hear that," she commiserated.

"There's a new cable station that shows marathons of the old eighties cartoons. You would love it! Beats the crap out of the stuff they make now. This shit is seriously inspired."

She shook her head. "Whatever. I'm going to make popcorn and chill in my room. You want some?"

He shook his head.

Tash went to the kitchen for a Diet Coke and tub of microwave popcorn before going to her room. She changed into her most worn-in cotton pajamas and crawled into bed, propped up against pillows. She cycled through the channels, searching for something to watch. She came across the end credits for *Rainbow Bright* and was curious enough to stop. *Jason's a trip. Too funny*, she giggled. Before she could change the station, *Jem and the Holograms* came on, catching her attention.

The aesthetic is fantastic, she thought, instantly riveted. *What a dope look. Such great colors. God, imagine this aesthetic in a live-action suspense flick. It would be like pop noir. J was right. This stuff is inspired.* After acclimating to the fashion and vibe, Tash became immersed in the story. The idea that one woman had two distinct personas, the glamorous Jem and the responsible, orphan-raising Jerrica, resonated deeply. *They keep acting as though Jerrica is real and Jem is an illusion, but they're both real. That's why Rio loves them both. He's kind of a douche, cheating or whatever, but he can't help it. Together, Jem and Jerrica are like the perfect woman. No wonder their superhuman, cyborg savior is named Synergy. Brilliant.*

She watched the *Jem and the Holograms* marathon for hours, relating to the two-persona lead character more than any real person she had ever known. They shared a bond. All night her thoughts vacillated from Jem to her conversation with Kyle. She kept replaying his words, "It's not who you are. That's how you acted to look like you were having fun." Every time there was a scene with Rio, she transposed Aidan's face on his. Eventually she fell asleep, with the glow of the television beaming like a halo around her face.

*

The next morning, she woke up to find her popcorn spilled across her bed and onto the floor. The television was still on and playing the final scene of *The Last Unicorn*. As Tash wiped the sleep from her eyes, the mythical creature admitted how she now lives with regret because she had to give up the man she loved to save herself. Tash sighed, searched for the remote control, and turned the television off. As she rolled out of bed, she stepped on some popcorn, making a crunching sound. She grabbed her robe and walked out into the hallway, peeking into Jason's room, where he was asleep on top of the sheets.

"Hey, what's up?"

"Sorry. Didn't mean to wake you."

"It's fine," he said as he rubbed his eyes. "You look tired. Come sit," he said, propping his pillows up and stretching his arms.

"I didn't get much sleep last night. Don't laugh, but I flipped on that cartoon station and they were running a marathon of *Jem and The Holograms.* I kind of binged on it."

"I wouldn't laugh. She's outrageous. Truly, truly, truly outrageous," he said with hearty laughter.

Tash grabbed a pillow and smacked him in the face with it. "Can I tell you something that will make me sound crazy?"

"Always."

"I kinda related to Jem, a lot. It's like she has this fun persona that this guy is attracted to, but it's not the only thing she is. She's a totally different person too."

"Yeah," Jason prodded.

"It made me think about Aidan. He said I hide behind a persona and need to figure out who I really am. And Kyle said something like that too. I think, I think…"

"Do you remember when we watched *Desperately Seeking Susan?*"

"Yeah."

"Well Sam and I were talking about it and I had a realization. They were in their twenties. Roberta, the Rosanna Arquette character stuck in a bad suburban marriage, she was our age. It's just the shoulder pads and makeup back then that made everyone look forty."

"And?" Tash probed.

"The movie is really about her trying to figure out who she is, not who people say she is or who she thinks she's supposed to be. It got me thinking that there's this time in your twenties, you know after college or whatever, but before whatever is supposed to happen actually happens."

"Before you figure your shit out," she said.

"Before you figure out who you are and what you're doing. Nobody tells you what the hell to do after school. It just feels like being suspended in air or something."

"Totally."

"I think it's like a period of time you have to struggle through to get to where you want to go."

Tash smiled.

"What?" Jason asked.

"It's like our Blue Period. Your friend doesn't have to off themselves. We kill off parts of ourselves; we have to. It's not really about grief or sadness, just being sort of lost," she said.

"But lost on the way to somewhere. Don't forget that. If we say goodbye to some version of who we are, it's only to become a better version."

"Jason, can I tell you something?"

"Anything."

"I fucked up. I miss Aidan."

"I know," he said, leaning over to hug her.

"I love him," she whispered in his ear.

"I know."

She pulled away and wiped tears from her eyes.

"Call him," Jason said.

"I will. But I think I need to do something for myself first. I may need to go out of town for a few days. Don't tell anyone, okay?"

He nodded. "But only if you text me every day so I know you're all good."

She smiled. "Love you."

"Love you back."

CHAPTER 11

As Jason was shaking the Lucky Charms box, hoping enough bits were stuck in the corners that when freed, he'd have enough for breakfast, Penelope came into the small kitchen. She opened the refrigerator and stared at the nearly bare shelves.

Jason put the cereal box down in defeat.

"Can you grab the milk?" he asked.

Penelope passed the milk cartoon, which contained a few last drops. He watched them drip into his crumb-lined bowl. Jason stood and ate the two bites of cereal before saying, "Pen, wasn't it your turn to go to the store?"

"I'm sorry. I forgot."

"That's not like you," he said, putting his empty bowl on the counter.

She shrugged.

"Pen?"

"I'll go to the store today. I'm really sorry."

"I don't care about the groceries. We can get takeout. I'm worried about you. What's going on? Whatever it is, you can tell me."

She took a deep breath and looked behind her to make sure they were alone.

"Tash isn't here. She had to go out of town for a few days," he assured her. "Pen, what is it?"

"Promise me you won't tell anyone."

"I promise."

"That includes Tash, especially Tash."

He nodded. "Okay, but why especially Tash?"

"I had an affair with a married man."

Jason's jaw dropped. "Holy shit!"

"Jason!"

"I'm sorry. But holy shit! That was literally the last thing I thought you were going to say."

"There's more."

Jason's eyes widened.

The man, the man I had a relationship with. I didn't know it at the time, but he's Tash's uncle, Kyle's dad."

"Holy shit!" he bellowed. He put his hand over his mouth and shook his head. "Sorry, oh God, I'm so sorry, Pen. It's just that is actually the last thing I thought you were going to say."

She looked down and shook her head.

Jason walked over and put his hand on her shoulder.

"Come on, let's make some coffee and sit down. You can tell me how this happened."

Soon Jason knew the entire story, from their initial meeting in Vermont to the "fateful" meeting months later, and everything that followed.

"I had no idea how hard your visits with your dad were. I'm so sorry. I feel like I got preoccupied with work and going out and wasn't paying attention. I guess I haven't been the best friend to you."

"It's not your fault. I never said anything. I think it made me too sad."

"Honestly, we both thought you were completely together, like a model citizen visiting your dad all the time and working so hard in school."

"I guess I kind of was for a while, but it was never easy," she said.

"Can I ask you something personal?"

She nodded.

"Were you in love?"

She shook her head. "I don't think so. I think I was just lonely more than anything and I wanted to change my life. It all just kind of happened. For a while, it felt comfortable. It makes what I did so much worse. I mean, if we weren't really in love there was no excuse."

"If you weren't in love, and you broke up, why are you struggling so much? I don't mean that in a judgmental way; I just mean I've noticed how upset you've been lately. Some days it looked like you were crying in your room. Are you crying over him?"

"No. I've been depressed and ashamed. Once it was over, letting him go didn't even hurt. It should have hurt, shouldn't it?"

"Isn't it better that it doesn't hurt?"

She shrugged. "I've been terrified that Tash will find out and hate me. On top of everything, I let school slide to be with him. Now, the one thing I was always good at is also a mess. I'm overwhelmed."

Jason leaned in and hugged her, gently rubbing her back. "It will be okay," he whispered.

"Thanks," she said as she pulled back.

"First of all, the school stuff will work out. You can get yourself back on track with some of those long library days you love. And as for Tash, I doubt she'll find out. But I do think you should tell her. It will make you feel better. Plus, I'm pretty sure she'll be glad to know you're human like the rest of us."

"You know how close she is with Kyle. I messed up his family."

"I doubt she'll see it that way. It's up to you. Tell her or don't, but either way you have to let it go and move on. I know this is new territory for you, but people fuck up all the time. You have to rebound."

"Once my classes ended, I think I was kind of in a free fall. After my mom died, I went to college and then straight to grad school. I did what I knew how to do: school. Being a student is so easy. There is always more you can study, more you can read, to fill the time. When my classes ended, I had to start figuring things out on my own. That's when I met Richard. I thought it was fate but he was really just something to fill my mind and my time. I needed somewhere to be, someone to meet, and something to focus on. I mean, why do you guys think I always handle all the household bills and everything?"

"Because you don't want the electric turned off and you're the only real grown-up here."

She smiled. "There is that. But I also need predictable ways to fill my days. I need a structure that I understand, which I realize makes me sound pathetic. But I mean, without classes to attend or a family to go home to, what am I supposed to do?"

"You're already home, and you're with your family. I'm your family. Tash is too, in her own, dysfunctional way."

"You don't have to say that."

"I mean it. I know we can be pretty self-absorbed, but that doesn't make us feel like family any less. Isn't that part of what life is? Creating your own place in the world, with your peeps, even if they're a mess."

She giggled. "Thanks. I guess I needed a reminder."

"How about we get out of this funk by going out? How does a movie sound?"

Penelope nodded. "By the way, where's Tash?"

*

After canceling on him the day before to spend time with Penelope, Jason met Sam at an Italian restaurant in Tribeca, promising to "make it up to him." As he approached the restaurant, he saw Sam waiting outside.

"Do they have a table?"

"I was thinking we could sit at the bar for a drink," Sam said.

"Sure."

They sat at the nearly empty bar and savored the smell of garlic bread wafting in the air.

"You won't believe all the drama going on right now," Jason said as he focused on the cocktail menu. "My roommates are both going through some seriously screwed up stuff with guys. I promised I wouldn't say anything, but..."

"Yeah, that's what your text said. Listen..."

"Do you want to share a carafe of the house red wine or should I just get a glass?"

"Jason, I need to talk to you," Sam said solemnly, placing his hand on the drink menu.

Jason put the menu down and swiveled his barstool to face Sam.

"What's up?"

"You and I have had a fun time together, but..."

Jason's jaw dropped. "Oh my God, you're blowing me off."

"I wanted to tell you in person. I just don't see this going anywhere."

"I don't get it," Jason said, mystified.

"We talked before, you know, about keeping it airy. I was coming out of a relationship when we met. I was flattered when you asked me out and, well, I never thought it would go anywhere. I'm not looking for a serious thing right now."

"So you used me to get over someone else?" Jason asked, trying to process what was happening.

"Not intentionally. But yes, you helped me move past someone else and now I think I need to be on my own for a while," Sam said, putting his hand on Jason's.

Jason was silent.

"Let me guess, no one has ever broken up with you before?" Sam asked.

"Ah, no. But I've never really done the exclusive thing before. It never occurred to me that if I wanted to be with someone, he might not want to be with me. God, that makes me sound like a jerk. I don't mean it that way."

Sam laughed. "I know you think that you were slumming it with me or doing some noble thing by dating someone so obviously beneath you."

"No, not at all. I thought we had a connection," Jason said, hurt. "Is that how little you think of me?"

"I'm sorry. That came out all wrong. I always trip over my words with you. Maybe I should go."

"Wait. Why did you make me come here to meet you? Why not just call?"

"Because I suspect that when you end things with someone, you just take off and leave them wondering. I wanted to show you it doesn't need to be that way. I don't mean to be condescending, but…"

"But what?"

Sam stood up. "I should go. Despite what you may think, I've enjoyed every minute with you. It was a lot of fun."

Fun? Is that all anyone thinks I'm good for?

Sam turned back to Jason. "For what it's worth, I wish you great success in figuring out how to use your platform to achieve what you really want."

As Jason watched Sam walk away, he thought, *Why is he so damn lovely? It would be so much easier to hate him if he were an asshole.*

When Jason got home, he headed straight for Penelope's room and tapped on the door.

"Yes?"

He opened the door and said, "I just got dumped. I'm inconsolable."

"Oh, no. Come sit. I'll get a carton of sorbet and you can tell me what happened."

"Can we skip the sorbet and order a pizza instead?" he asked as he flopped on her bed.

"Of course."

*

A couple of days later, Tash returned. She wheeled her suitcase past Jason's room, peeking in to find him watching talk shows.

"Hey."

"You're back!"

"Yeah. What did I miss?"

"Oh sweetie, we had our own drama for a change."

"What's wrong? Why the *Sally Jessy* reruns?"

"Sam broke up with me."

"Oh, honey. Let me go put my bag away and I'll be right back for cuddles. We can talk about what an ugly douche he is."

Jason smiled. "Glad you're back."

*

As Tash finished sending a text, she turned to find Penelope standing in her doorway.

"Oh, hey Pen. I was just going to go check on Jason. He's pretty upset."

"Yeah, I know all about Sam. Listen, I really need to talk to you. It's important."

Tash widened her eyes, waiting.

"I've been working myself up to this and I'm afraid if I don't…" She trailed off.

"Is this about the bills? I promise I'll get you my share."

She shook her head. "No. It's just that, well, I wasn't going to tell you but Jason thought I should and, well…"

"Pen, I was just on a plane for like six hours. What is it? Spit it out."

"You may want to sit down for this."

Tash sat on the edge of her bed and Penelope told her everything, avoiding unnecessary details.

"Ewww! Gross," Tash said, squeezing her eyes shut in disgust.

"I'm so sorry, Tash. I had no idea who he was. I would never do anything to hurt you or anyone you care about."

"I'm not mad at you," Tash said.

"You're not?"

"No. I'm shocked and grossed out, but not mad. You didn't know, and it's not like I've never slept with the wrong guy. At least now I see why Dick is short for Richard."

"Are you going to tell Kyle?"

"No way. Listen, his parents have a totally screwed up marriage anyway. You probably did them a favor. I mean, if he wasn't getting it for years, you gave him what he needed. Otherwise he'd probably leave my aunt. She's a total whack job."

Penelope took a deep breath. "I've been such a wreck, terrified you'd never forgive me."

"You worry too much. But what the fuck did you see in my uncle? He's so totally unappealing, except that he's rich, but you don't care about that stuff."

"He was nice to me. He listened to me. I guess it was sort of like a fantasy. I've always been good at reality but I wanted an escape so I let myself believe it was fate. I've been kind of lost, trying to figure out where I fit in."

Tash smiled knowingly. "Don't worry. I get it. It's your Blue Period."

"My what?"

*

Tash and Penelope joined Jason in his bed, sandwiching him in the middle.

"Cheer up, J. I mean, how long was it going to last with a makeup artist anyway? He knows all of your flaws," Tash said.

Jason sighed. "I know. I just can't believe he dumped me. And I ate pizza, like the really greasy delivery kind!"

"How could you let him eat that?" Tash scolded Penelope.

"He needed comfort. I didn't think a healthy fruit snack was going to do the trick."

Jason and Tash burst into laughter.

"Pen, you made a joke!" Tash exclaimed.

Penelope shook her head.

"Maybe all the sex with my nasty old uncle loosened you up!" Tash continued through laughter.

"Oh, shut up," Penelope said, burying her face in her hands.

"Seriously, Jason, can you believe our virtuous little roomie was going all around town screwing someone?"

Jason laughed. "She's not a girl anymore."

"Honestly Pen, we thought you'd be chaste forever. If it weren't for who you did it with, I'd be impressed!"

Penelope grabbed a pillow and hit Tash in the head.

Jason, now hysterical, chimed in with, "Well, this took my mind off Sam."

As the laughter subsided, Penelope said, "I really missed this. You know, hanging out together."

"Yeah, sorry I've been so wrapped up in my own shit," Tash said.

"We love you for that, honey," Jason said.

Penelope nodded. "Hey, so where were you anyway, Tash?"

"First I visited my parents for two days to beg for some money and then I flew to LA. Listen, guys. I have big news."

*

That afternoon there was a knock on Tash's bedroom door. She opened it and came face-to-face with Aidan.

"Jason let me in. I got your text."

Her eyes lit up. "Thanks for coming over. Come in," she said, closing the door behind him.

"Do you want to sit down?" she asked as she sat cross-legged on her bed.

"I'm good here," he said, leaning against the door.

"You never called or texted, not even once," she said.

He raised his eyebrows.

She sighed. "I know, I know. It was on me."

He lowered his chin.

"Listen, I'm sorry about that night, how I acted."

"You really hurt me."

"I know. I wish I could take it all back."

"Tell me why. What was really going on?"

She took a long, slow breath. "I've never had a relationship where someone treated me well, until you. I guess I self-sabotaged. Maybe you were right and I don't believe I deserve good things."

"Did something happen that night?"

"Some guy in the bathroom basically called me a whore and then someone offered me ecstasy."

"Assholes."

"No, you don't understand. A few years ago, I probably would have screwed that guy, and I would have taken whatever crap I could get my hands on, to party. I was a mess and I didn't care."

"So it's good because it shows how you've evolved," Aidan said supportively.

"You don't understand. Back then I did a lot of bad stuff, and bad stuff happened to people, including me."

Aidan sat next to her on the bed. "We're not responsible for everything that happens to us."

"I feel like I brought bad shit on myself. It's hard to shake that," she said.

"Then don't shake it. Deal with it head on, and then let it go."

"Aidan…"

"Yeah?" he said as he took her hand.

"I missed you so much."

He smiled brightly. "That's all I was waiting for, beauty queen."

She looked down, blushing. "Harold is missing. I saw him a couple of weeks ago and I snapped at him. I was having a horrible day and now he's missing and the last thing I said to him was mean."

"I'm sorry. Maybe the cops chased him off and he'll come back."

"Maybe."

"So are you coming or going?" Aidan asked, gesturing to the suitcase.

"Both, actually."

He knitted his brow.

"Aidan, you were right about so much. I was stuck, afraid to take a chance on myself. I don't want to be bored or restless. I want to go after things."

He smiled.

"But you weren't right about everything. I am a person who likes to have fun and to be carefree. That's not an act; it's a part of who I am. If you can't accept that…"

He squeezed her hand. "I love that about you. Always have. I mean, I'm a deejay for a reason. I like the lighter side too." She leaned in and kissed him softly. He took the back of her head in his hand and returned her kiss with passion. "I love you. You know that, right?" he asked as he pulled back, centimeters from her face.

She nodded.

"So you never told me, what's with the suitcase?"

"One of my professors always promised to hook me up with an internship at Paramount Studios. I finally took him up on it and flew to LA for an interview. They hired me on the spot."

He smiled. "That's amazing."

"It's actually a pretty crappy job and I'll mostly be getting people coffee, but if I'm going to have a crappy job I figured it should be where I can meet people who can teach me."

"That's awesome," he said.

"My bigger plan is to go to grad school and get my MFA in cinematography. I want to make films or at least do something related to film. I missed the application period but I'm going to apply for next year. UCLA has a kickass program. Even if I don't get in, there are a bunch of schools in the area."

Aidan looked down. "That's really great. Truly," he said softly.

"I was thinking: I know you're established here, but if you could move from Chicago to New York, can't you go from New York to LA?"

He looked at her, grinning like a Cheshire cat.

"I mean, there's a huge deejay scene in LA, right? At the very least, there must be a Forever 21 or frat party you can spin at. What do you think?" she asked with a smirk.

"Well, they do have coconuts there."

She smiled.

"Do you remember?" he asked.

"I remember."

AFTERWORD: CONNECTIONS BETWEEN
BLUE AND *LOW-FAT LOVE*

When I first wrote the character of Tash in *Low-Fat Love*, I didn't like her. She wasn't the kind of person I would typically want to be friends with. Petulant, spoiled, superficial, attention-seeking – these are all ways one could describe her. I loved taking this unlikable character and placing her at the center of the narrative. While she can still be described as bratty, entitled, and so on, like all of us, she's multidimensional and complex. Tash was particularly interesting for me to explore as a social scientist turned writer because she embodies contradictions. She's at once self-absorbed and deeply caring, superficial and engaged, lazy and passionate, dismissive and protective, and while in one moment she is oblivious to her privileges, in another, she challenges hypocrisy. Although she's often careless with her words, she also has a remarkable capacity to accept people as they are. Through her struggles to integrate all parts of herself, I have been reminded of the importance of self-awareness and self-acceptance. I hope Tash, as well as Penelope and Jason, also remind us that people are often struggling with things we know nothing about. As the famed sociologist Erving Goffman might say, much of what we see "front stage" is a result of what's going on "back stage," which we aren't privy to.

Low-Fat Love influenced *Blue* well beyond Tash. When I wrote *Low-Fat Love*, I couldn't have predicted its success. I never thought anyone would read it. The response to the book still surprises me, and even surprises my publisher. It hit a nerve in a way that I could never have anticipated. Since the release of the first edition in 2011, countless people have sent me notes and sought me out at book talks and conferences to tell me stories of their own low-fat love and how they related to the novel. I'm humbled to hear these stories. As a novel, it can rightly be interpreted in many ways, a strength of the form. It isn't my place in encounters with readers to impose my viewpoint. However, one comment I've frequently heard is how awfully the protagonist in *Low-Fat Love* was treated by her boyfriend (indeed, the other female lead has a destructive relationship with her father). Readers often blame the men of *Low-Fat Love* for their damaging effect on the female characters. This is a perfectly valid interpretation. There are certainly male characters in the book who treat women poorly. But for me, the story is much more about how the women treat themselves and their own participation in negative relationships. When I started writing *Blue*, I decided there would be positive male characters, like Aidan and Jason, but the female characters would struggle anyway. In this respect, *Blue* and *Low-Fat Love* are different points on a continuum, both showing that our primary relationship is with ourselves.

As readers of both books may see, *Blue* has many nods to *Low-Fat Love*, most of which happened organically as I was writing. I don't want to unpack them all for you, but one example is the colorful feathers falling around Tash and Aidan at the club, which is reminiscent of Melville's "chicken feathers." There are many other references found in both books, from pivotal events to items of pop culture and food. Thematically, suicide, grief, and sexual assault are all referenced. The character of Sarah Cohen, the feminist historian, also makes a very brief appearance in all three of my novels. I think of her as a version of myself, watching and documenting. Finally, pop culture provides the subtext for both novels. Unlike *Low-Fat Love*, *Blue* doesn't provide a critique of pop culture, but is more of a celebration of it. So while in *Low-Fat Love* characters often consume stereotypical pop culture and then show us its negative effects through interior dialogue, in *Blue*, characters are often imaged in the "glow" of light from television or movie screens, their own stories illuminated by the stories of popular culture.

For those interested in the emergence of Tash in *Low-Fat Love*, please read the excerpt at the end of this book, which is when she first appears along with her cousin, Kyle.

Love and Light,
Patricia

SUGGESTED CLASSROOM USE

1. *Blue* suggests we can all become different versions of ourselves. Explore this topic in relation to any of the central characters. What about with yourself or your friends?

2. The use of fiction allows for the exploration of the "inner worlds" of characters through techniques such as interior monologue. How did this technique help uncover the identity issues the characters were struggling with?

3. What did the dialogue reveal about how the characters relate to each other? For example, pick a scene of Tash and Jason speaking or Tash and Aidan, and discuss what we learn about them by examining the content and the ways in which they speak to each other.

4. The issue of coping with all forms of abuse comes up in different ways in the book, from Sam being harassed on the streets of his hometown, to Aidan being beaten up in high school, and Tash remembering her sexual assault. How are these issues reflected on your college campus?

5. Pop culture is used as a series of signposts throughout the book in order to show the larger context in which people build their identities and make sense of their lives. Highlight all the pop culture references in the book and jot down your ideas of the "pop culture world" painted. Pick a couple of the pop culture references and explain how they impact a character's thinking or reflect something about them.

6. Issues relating to social class, the high cost of education, privilege, race, sexual orientation, and gender pop up throughout the book. Pick a couple of these examples to reflect on from a social science perspective.

7. Sociologically, *Blue* explores the "front stage" and "back stage" of the main characters' lives. Find a few examples of this in the book.

8. *Blue* suggests that friendships are invaluable to our lives, influencing our sense of self and our other relationships. Write about this topic using examples from the book.

CREATIVE WRITING ASSIGNMENTS

1. Select one of the minor characters and write his/her story.

2. Select one of the characters and fast-forward five years. Write a short story based on where you think they are now.

3. Pick a scene written in the narrator's voice and rewrite it with one of the main characters as the narrator.

4. Pick a scene featuring Tash and Aidan and switch the perspective, so that we see things from Aidan's point of view. What does his interior dialogue reveal?

5. Write an alternative ending to *Blue*.

QUALITATIVE RESEARCH ACTIVITIES

1. Select several scenes and perform discourse or conversation analysis on the dialogue. For example, use the scene of Tash and Aidan's big fight or Tash and Jason talking about people being lost in their twenties.

2. Conduct a content analysis of the pop-culture items in the book.

EXCERPT FROM LOW-FAT LOVE: EXPANDED ANNIVERSARY EDITION

(the opening of chapter 6)

Kyle Goldwyn was not an average seventeen-year-old. Despite his mother's not-so-secret anxiety that he may be below average in almost every conceivable way, Kyle was, surreptitiously, quite exceptional. He was enormously perceptive. He not only saw things that other people seemed to miss, but he saw them in remarkable ways.

At the age of three, an older and larger boy bullied him at preschool. When Kyle built a block fortress, the other boy came and kicked it down while mocking him. One day the boy pushed Kyle off a swing, causing him to badly scrape his knees. After Janice repeatedly yelled at the director of the preschool, threatening to sue if her son was hurt again (she made such a scene that the woman forever cringed at the sight of her), Janice told Kyle, "Ignore the boy. He's a loser."

Kyle replied, "I think he must be very unhappy."

Janice rolled her eyes and feared that Kyle was a wimp. When he was eight years old, a discussion about Christmas in his third grade class prompted him to ask his mother why Jesus Christ was killed. Only partly hearing the question she answered, "That's what the Bible teaches, that's all. You don't have to agree if you don't."

Kyle responded, "I think Jesus Christ must have been very special. Maybe his ideas were so special that they frightened people."

Janice was preoccupied with opening junk mail and just said, "Uh huh."

Kyle ran upstairs to his room, where he spent the rest of the afternoon lying on his bed and wondering what made good people afraid. During the next several years as Janice schlepped him from museum to museum hoping to "make him interesting," Kyle began to see the world through different lenses. When Janice got the free audio headset tour so that Kyle could "properly learn about the great art," he always muted it. He looked at the paintings, sculptures, and photographs and tried to imagine where the artist was from, how they grew up, how they came to see the world, and how much of that vision lay before him, lopped off in a frame. This process made him wonder about different cultures and how they produce different kinds of people. He wondered where innovation came from, why some people's work seemed derivative and others stood on its own, unable to be defined or judged. He came to see beauty in her many guises, which so too made him clearly see her falsehoods.

Kyle was keenly aware of people's emotional centers, as if he could almost feel them immediately. A kind soul, he used this skill only to the advantage of others, never his own. This gift of perception helped him in innumerable ways, not the least of which was related to his mother. Of all the things that Kyle could perceive in his environment, what he saw most clearly was when there was a need for silence. Therefore, Kyle Goldwyn knew that the greatest kindness he could show his mother was not to show her all the things he saw, and so he didn't.

Although quiet and not terribly good looking in the traditional sense, Kyle was not considered unattractive by his peers. Contrary to his parents' assumption, he had dated several girls (including fooling around with a few and sleeping with two). He had many friends at school, and more importantly, had no enemies. Outside of school, he spent most of his time with his best friend, Sam.

Kyle and Sam hung out in Central Park playing cards; they went to music stores and browsed old vinyl; they walked around the Village, talking about the evils of organized religion or politics (they were both fiercely on the left, though unimpressed by most politicians and surprisingly missing the idealism often characterized by leftie youth); they went to parties at friends' houses or met girls at the movies; and most often, they went to Sam's place and watched movies. Kyle frequently crashed on a small futon in Sam's room. Sam lived in a tiny, two-bedroom apartment with his mother, Melanie, a paralegal at a Wall Street law firm. She had long blonde hair, and Kyle thought she was incredibly beautiful and looked far too young to be a mother, though he knew not to mention this to Sam.

Sometimes they stopped by the NYU dorms to see Kyle's cousin, Natashya. Neither Kyle nor Natashya ever told their parents, but they had become close friends during those brutal family vacation weeks. They texted every week (sometimes daily) and hung out at least once a month since Natashya (Tash as Kyle and Kyle alone called her) moved to New York. When one of them had a problem they needed to talk about, they met at their favorite boisterous deli, where they always waited until a booth opened up. They shared a platter of blueberry cheese blintzes and a pot of weak coffee, which they always complained about. Although she looked naïve with a freckled face and preppy clothes that stood out in the artsy punk crowds in her neighborhood, Natashya was a rebel. She used to tell Kyle that she was "sexually free" when he questioned why she always seemed to be "hooking up with some random guy." In response, she teased him that he was just uptight because they were cousins. He thought that she was a little too free. He feared that she didn't know how foolish she could look. Natashya also had a fake ID that she used to buy beer for Kyle and Sam. Kyle and Sam never drank more than one or two cans. From time to time, she also smoked a joint. Sam always took a hit or two but Kyle never did. This wasn't because he was a "straight edge," as Natashya would say while giggling, but rather because he knew that if there were ever an emergency, one of them needed to be sober. He only trusted himself with that responsibility.

Kyle was acutely aware of Tash's propensity to morph free-spiritedness into a lack of consideration for others. He didn't let it bother him until Halloween. Natashya invited Kyle and Sam to a party at an underground club. She insisted that they dress in costume. When they arrived at her dorm, both made up to look like mimes, Kyle immediately noticed that Tash seemed a little out of it. Her eyes didn't focus when she offered them a beer while she finished styling her hair. He figured she had smoked a bit. She was wearing a Playboy bunny costume, complete with a white fluffy tail, white fishnet stockings, and stripper-style white patent leather stilettos. With her innocent face covered in makeup and her very fine light brown hair long and stick straight, Sam thought she looked hot. She had a Lindsay Lohan look. Kyle thought that a long dress revealing one bare shoulder was far sexier than her hookeresque ensemble, but he kept this thought to himself to avoid being teased and called uptight, which he wasn't. Tash was too special to distract the eye in such cliché ways.

"What do you think?" she asked, throwing her arms up in one of her over-the-top model poses.

"You look awesome," Sam said enthusiastically.

"Weeell?" she asked, looking at Kyle.

"I think you're more beautiful than you know," he answered.

She smiled brightly and said, "Let's roll; cabs will be tough tonight."

Three hours later Kyle and Sam were getting bored. The large red club decked out in an excess of black streamers and hanging paper skeletons was massively crowded, and over time, the heavy synthesizer sounds of the techno music grated on their nerves.

"Come on, let's get out of here, man," Sam said.

"Yeah, ok. I have to find Tash to tell her we're going and to make sure she's ok getting a cab on her own."

"I'll wait here."

"Ok," Kyle shouted as he made his way through the crowded dance floor to the last place he had seen her, which was over an hour ago. He wandered around, squinting when the strobe lights flashed in his face. He stood outside of the women's bathroom for fifteen minutes, thinking that if she were in there she'd have to pass him when she left. He sent her three text messages without reply. Tash was nowhere to be found. Eventually, he made his way back to Sam.

"Hey dude, what happened to you? I didn't think you were coming back."

"Can't find Tash. I don't like just leaving her here. She's probably wasted."

"She brought us here man. I'm sure she can handle herself. Let's go to my place. My mom's out with that jackass again. We can do whatever we want."

Kyle scanned the room one more time before acquiescing, "Yeah, ok, let's get out of here."

From the subway, Kyle sent Tash two more text messages. Never drifting off for more than an hour at a time he checked his phone religiously all night in hopes of a reply.

The next day at five in the afternoon, Natashya finally texted:

```
Hey. Sorry 2 worry. Met a friend. Hope
you had fun. Hugs, T.
```

Kyle wasn't the type to get angry and certainly not one to hold a grudge, but something in him shifted ever so slightly that night. He never mentioned it to her or to anyone.

*

Please pick up *Low-Fat Love: Expanded Anniversary Edition* from Sense Publishers to learn more about:

- Tash, including the fateful New Year's Eve party
- The origins of Pete Rice's *The Lost Notebooks*
- Richard's twenty-year marriage

And meet the characters who started it all, Prilly Greene and Janice Goldwyn. Here's a synopsis of the book:

Low-Fat Love unfolds over three seasons as Prilly Greene and Janice Goldwyn, adversarial editors at a New York press, experience personal change relating to the men, and absence of women, in their lives. Ultimately, each woman is pushed to confront her own image of herself, exploring her insecurities, the stagnation in her life, her attraction to men who withhold their support, and her reasons for having settled for low-fat love.

Prilly lives in between who she is and who she longs to be. Prilly falls for Pete Rice, an unemployed, ever sexy, and curiously charming aspiring graphic novelist. Prilly thinks she is finally experiencing the big life she always sought but feared was beyond her grasp because she was "in the middle" (not beautiful nor ugly, not greatly talented nor totally hopeless – someone who could work for it). Pete's unconventional, free-spirited views on relationships unsettle Prilly, ultimately causing her to unravel over the course of their on-again-off-again love affair. Meanwhile, Janice, a workaholic, feminist in-name-only editor, overburdens Prilly, her underling, with busywork and undercuts Prilly's professional identity. Janice's regimented life is set on a new course when her alcoholic father is injured in a car accident and she is forced to face her own demons.

Along with Prilly and Janice, the cast of characters' stories are interwoven throughout and eventually connect in the third and final section of the book. The offbeat characters include: Melville Wicket, Pete's awkward friend who lives one beat outside of the moment; Jacob, Melville's younger, pothead brother; Kyle Goldwyn, Janice's seventeen-year-old son who appears ordinary in every way but is actually quite extraordinary; and Tash, Kyle's wild-child, flighty, sexpot cousin who attends NYU and ends up dating Jacob. In the end, momentum builds as the characters struggle to escape the consequences of their decisions. Unexpected events cause changes in the characters that appear minor but carry significant implications for their futures.

ABOUT THE AUTHOR

Patricia Leavy, PhD is an independent scholar and novelist (formerly Associate Professor of Sociology, Chair of Sociology & Criminology, and Founding Director of Gender Studies at Stonehill College). She received her PhD in sociology from Boston College. She is widely considered an international leader in the fields of arts-based research and qualitative inquiry. Her nineteen published books include *Method Meets Art: Arts-Based Research Practice* (first and second editions, Guilford Press), *The Oxford Handbook of Qualitative Research* (Oxford University Press), *Fiction as Research Practice* (Left Coast Press), *Essentials of Transdisciplinary Research* (Left Coast Press), *Gender & Pop Culture: A Text-Reader* (co-edited with Adrienne Trier-Bieniek, Sense Publishers), and the best-selling novels *Low-Fat Love* (first and second editions, Sense Publishers) and *American Circumstance* (Sense Publishers). She is series creator and editor for five book series, including *Social Fictions*, *Teaching Gender*, *Teaching Race and Ethnicity*, *Teaching Writing* (for Sense Publishers), and *Understanding Qualitative Research* (for Oxford University Press). Known for her commitment to public scholarship, she is frequently called on by the national news media and has regular blogs for *The Huffington Post*, *The Creativity Post*, and *We Are the Real Deal*. Examiner called her "the high priestess of pop feminism." She received the New England Sociological Association 2010 New England Sociologist of the Year Award, the American Creativity Association 2014 Special Achievement Award, the American Educational Research Association Qualitative SIG 2015 Egon Guba Memorial Keynote Lecture Award, and the International Congress of Qualitative Inquiry 2015 Special Career Award (she is the youngest recipient). Dr. Leavy delivers invited talks and keynote lectures at universities, private events, and national and international conferences. Please visit www.patricialeavy.com for more information.

Printed in the United States
By Bookmasters